Selfhood and Redemption in Blake's *Songs*

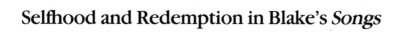

Selfhood and Redemption in Blake's *Songs*

Harold Pagliaro

THE PENNSYLVANIA STATE UNIVERSITY PRESS
University Park and London

I acknowledge the kindness of the Harry Elkins Widener Memorial Collection, Harvard University, for permission to reproduce illustrations from one of its copies of Blake's *Songs of Innocence and of Experience;* of The University of Wisconsin Press for permission to make use of portions of my Preface to *Studies in Eighteenth-Century Culture,* vol. 2, *Irrationalism in the Eighteenth Century* (Cleveland: The Press of Case Western Reserve University), 1972; of Martin Dodsworth, editor of *English,* published by Oxford University Press for the English Association, for permission to quote from my article "Blake's 'Self-Annihilation': Aspects of Its Function in the *Songs,*" *English* 30, 137 (Summer 1981): 117–46.

Library of Congress Cataloging-in-Publication Data

Pagliaro, Harold E.
    Selfhood and redemption in Blake's *Songs.*

    Includes index.
    1. Blake, William, 1757–1827. Songs of innocence.
2. Blake, William, 1757–1827. Songs of experience.
3. Blake, William, 1757–1827—Knowledge—Psychology.
4. Self in literature. 5. Redemption in literature.
6. Psychology in literature. I. Title.
PR4144.S63P28 1986   821'.7   86–43162
ISBN 0-271-00603-X

To my mother, Linda Ricci,
and to the memory of
my father, Harry E. Pagliaro

Contents

Preface

This book intends to offer a reading of *Songs of Innocence and of Experience* as a basis for a more immediate sense of Blake's psychology of redemption than is generally available in the scholarship. Most readers associate Blake's redemption with the prophecies, for it is there that he tells us how Milton and Albion/Christ are saved. Like most readers, I have found the prophecies rich in evidence that gives meaning to words like "Selfhood," "Self-examination," and "Self-annihilation," that is, to words closely connected with Blake's idea of redemption. But as a reader of the long poems, I have been a spectator of the events represented there more than a participant in them, and my sense for Milton's salvation, for example, has been proportionately abstract.

It is generally understood that even excepting "To Tirzah," the *Songs* and the prophecies are compatible, together representing consistent ideas and attitudes. And many scholars, including Damon, Wicksteed, Frye, Gleckner, Erdman, and Bloom, in various ways state or imply that the pattern of spiritual development identified by the terms "Innocence," "Experience," and "Higher Innocence" obtains in both the *Songs* and the prophecies. But no one, as far as I know, has considered that the songs, taken together might be intelligible in their psychological particulars rather than in a perspective defined by social criticism, by irony, or by some derivative of Christian doctrine. The argument that follows shows that Blake's *Songs* not only anticipate the redemption generally associated with the later poems, but they also make it available in such psychological detail as to give new meaning to Selfhood, Self-examination, and Self-annihilation, and to encourage the reader to participate in the redemptive process.

For what emerges in this reading of the *Songs* is not only a consistent human psychology, despite the great variety of intellectual and aesthetic capacity among the characters, but also a keen sense of the dynamics of the continuous process of psychological development from Selfhood's origins to the recognition that the death of Jesus is not understood until it becomes our own. It is a recognition that results in our psychological disorientation and renewal, an internal event that Blake requires of us all. I believe this identification of the dynamics of process makes a new dimension of the *Songs* systematically available. It also provides a basis for speculating about a variety of matters related to redemption in Blake's universe—matters such as the nature of self, the formation and the uses of Selfhood, the relationship of individual to universal being, the value of will in Self-examination, and the limits of Self-annihilation.

This reading also points to a way of relating the *Songs* to the prophecies. As I try to show in the last chapter, Blake's changing vision of the natural world follows a clear progression from early to late poems. The *Songs* offer us psychological particularity, and the prophecies, the form and clarity of a whole vision; these at least are the characteristics of each most obviously available to us. I believe I could not have read the *Songs* as I have done without the broad guidance of the prophetic books. But having read the *Songs* in a way made possible by the long poems, I am convinced that the reading helps us to see what the prophecies by themselves have not often shown—a sense for the human particulars of their actions.

Songs of Innocence and of Experience may be regarded as the individuated prelude to the prophecies, whose setting is the universal mind. Broadly considered, *Songs* are located in the natural world of death, whereas the prophecies are located in the unending world of the divine humanity. Although we may be aware that the two are interpenetrating, it has not been clear that the psychological particulars of the *Songs* have been available for increasing our understanding of the relationship between the two. Like some of his characters in *Songs of Experience*, Blake seems to have glimpsed eternity in departures from his vision as a natural man; having crossed the threshold many times, no doubt, he came to prefer the interior mental geography in which he located the action of the long poems. Though in making this choice he takes his reader to a world in which the particulars and continuities of human experience are not often apparent, he must have carried a knowledge of such particulars with him. Indeed, his very sense for the implications of such particulars may be said to have prepared the way for his movement from *Songs* to prophecies. And he must have understood his readers to share his knowledge of particulars as they read his prophetic works. I believe my reading of the *Songs* may help to provide the knowledge, by giving full shape to the dynamic psychological process represented there. I do not offer a reading of the prophecies, but my last chapter considers various connections between the *Songs* and the long poems.

The argument that follows shows that death figures not incidentally and intermittently in Blake's poetry, and not primarily as the symbolic crux of his interest in Jesus, but as the psychological basis of his view of redemption. In fact, Blake's capacity to look at death less fleetingly than most of us may be said to account both for his ability to understand how the rationalizing mind of the natural man operates and to understand what it takes for such a mind to rid itself of error. This capacity, I shall argue, makes Blake unique among the English romantics, who, except for him, one way or another qualify their most liberating vision of things, either by incorporating into that vision their persistent sense of mortality or by considering mortality in opposition to it. Blake's vision, on the contrary, moves through and beyond mortality.

My readings of Blake's *Songs* rely on David Erdman's text. They make no attempt to weigh the consequences of variant orderings, inclusions, and omissions, except for the reading of "To Tirzah," where the issue stood in my path. I shall simply note here that my argument is strengthened by Blake's transposition of "The Little Girl Lost" and "The Little Girl Found," "The School Boy," and "The Voice of the Ancient Bard" from *Songs of Innocence* to *Songs of Experience,* and by his replacement of "A Divine Image" with "The Human Abstract."

The few of Blake illustrations in this volume are intended as a convenience to the reader; they were chosen to help clarify interpretations that might otherwise have left questions unanswered in the reader's mind. Whenever possible, one should consult a full set of illustrations in which the *Songs* are set, preferably those reproduced in color, as slides or in book form.

My hope is that I have been able to show my reader a recognizable Blake under a new aspect. He is a psychologist who quickens a sense of the mind's need to build and use Selfhood and then to find opportunities for annihilating it.

Acknowledgments

I am happy to acknowledge my debt to Swarthmore College, which supported me during a year of leave from administrative and teaching duties in 1979–80, when I did much of the research for this book, and to the National Endowment for the Humanities, which awarded me a senior fellowship during 1983–84, when I drafted it.

I am also happy to mention my obligation to the following libraries: the Bodleian Library, the British Museum, the Columbia University Library, the Library of Congress, the New York Public Library, the University of Pennsylvania Library, the Library Company of Philadelphia, and the Swarthmore College Library. I wish to thank the representatives of these institutions who helped me with my work.

The debts I owe to the many colleagues who encouraged me to produce the book are less easily acknowledged because they helped me in various complicated ways. I shall be able to mention only some of them here. Carl Woodring many years ago accepted my paper "Death and Transformation in English Romantic Poetry" for a reading to Group IX at an MLA convention, and so supported my interest in a subject of which the present study is an outgrowth. The Publications Committee of the American Society for Eighteenth-Century Studies invited me to edit the Annual Proceedings for 1972, *Irrationalism in the Eighteenth Century,* providing me with an opportunity to explore some of the historical antecedents of the English romantics' interest in the subject of death in the preface to the volume. Martin

Dodsworth, editor of *English,* offered useful suggestions about my article "Blake's 'Self-Annihilation': Aspects of Its Function in the *Songs*" and accepted it for publication in 1981, making the thesis of this study available in abbreviated form. Robert F. Gleckner and Mark Greenberg, who have edited a volume on approaches to teaching the *Songs,* soon to be published by The Modern Language Association, have included my essay "Teaching Blake's Psychology of Redemption in *Songs*"; moreover, both read the manuscript and made many useful suggestions, Mark Greenberg being especially helpful by commenting not only in the written word but in live discourse too. David Bromwich also commented extensively on almost every page of the manuscript, reading so closely as to live through the book with me. Finally, David V. Erdman (who has encouraged me over the years) and Anne Kostelanetz Mellor, the book's most recent readers, have been supportive and very helpful with their suggestions. For all this assistance I am deeply grateful.

1

Contrary States and Their Psychological Continuum

If one reads each poem in *Songs of Innocence and of Experience* for evidence of the chief character's functioning psychology in the world of the poem, one finds that a pattern of redemption emerges for the *Songs* as a whole. Though such critics as Frye, Gleckner, and Bloom are aware of a gradual progress in the *Songs* from Innocence to Experience, and with the ideal of organized Innocence beyond, they rely on a knowledge of Blake's redemptive process as it is identified in the prophecies and other works for crucial elements of their critical structure of the *Songs*.[1] In this method, Blake's universe is identified in fairly large terms derived from all of his poetry and prose, and then the *Songs* are analyzed with fairly extensive reference to that rich and suggestive context of meaning. I doubt that anyone who has read all of Blake can avoid being affected by a sense for the whole as he reads the *Songs,* and I am not about to recommend an exclusive address to the *Songs.* Nor do I wish to suggest that the readings produced by Frye, Gleckner, Bloom, and others, along with readings that adduce a special context in which to consider the *Songs*—the idea of pastoral, or the eighteenth-century debate about education and childhood[2]—are not accurate and extremely useful to students of Blake. I wish only to claim that reading the *Songs* from the "inside," to a much greater extent than has been usual, with an eye to the functioning psychology of the chief characters, will yield evidence for defining not only various states of Innocence and states of Experience the *Songs* have been shown to represent but also the psychology underlying the passage from one to the other and beyond. Though it is a commonplace for criticism about the *Songs* to say that a character is in this or that degree of Innocence or Experience, no study has concerned itself with the psychological process *as* process, of movement from one state to another, a process I believe to be evidenced in the *Songs.*

The comprehensiveness of religious archetypal structures to which Blake's works have been convincingly referred, in terms so full and adequate it seems impossible to enlarge the territories of Blake's meaning, has proved a blessing. The works of Damon, Frye, Frosch, Fox, and Gallant come most immediately to mind.[3] But the very excellence of this scholarship, which has guided us all, may obscure a crucial issue and mislead us to a doubtful conclusion. I believe it may be too generally assumed that the paradigm of redemption in Blake's work—Selfhood formed, Selfhood examined, Selfhood annihilated—is amply understood. But the combination of Hebrew prophetic, Christian, and psychological terms used to discuss the paradigm, though identifying it well enough, has not articulated it in terms most likely to move us so that we may be said to share in its operation rather than to observe it. I believe such terms are available and that they derive from the psychology out of which states and changing states of characters in the *Songs* are generated.

It was not until Blake wrote *Milton* that he used the terms "Selfhood," "Self-examination," "Self-annihilation." By that time he had very clear notions about the redemptive process these terms represent, notions heavily qualified by his sense for the difficulty of its success. He knew the mind to be a complex instrument, so profoundly and unconsciously committed to saving the life of the body in which it was located that its other love, eternity, seemed remote. Blake's poetical development from the *Songs* to the long poems, by way of the shorter prophecies, seems to be in part the record of his earlier recognition of this dark complexity at the same time that it is a new means of giving it shape. In the prophecies he works to characterize redemption in universal terms, making use of characters bigger than life. We understand the general psychology of their spiritual quest, but so far, at least, we understand much more abstractly than we would wish to. This is not the place to argue the precise reasons for Blake's change of poetic mode. Indeed there is probably no very solid evidence on which to base such an argument. The relevant fact for my present purpose is that his epic poems, which presumably give an appropriate magnitude to his perennial concern—humanity's redemption—also remove it from the world of the *Songs,* in which we encounter characters who may help us to recognize it immediately. Almost as complicated as *Milton* in their totality, the *Songs* are nevertheless made up of separated elements, the individual poems, which we may at a first level regard discretely. Each one with its illustration treats a psychological state that both masks and reveals the mind passing through that state or arrested by it. Each one provides us with an opportunity for seeing such operations as the formation of Selfhood, the function of Selfhood, the reflexive regard of Selfhood, the failed attempt to circumvent Selfhood, the partial or momentary dissolution of Selfhood, the vision beyond Selfhood. (The many studies of the *Songs,* accurate though they may be in their readings of individual poems, treat them with what may be too heavy an emphasis on their representation of divided entities in want of an act of union—the marriage of child and adult, lamb and tiger, world and otherworld, day and night. There can be no doubt that the *Songs* imply such unions through the juxtaposition of these and other polarities, which are essential to our understanding them. But underlying the poles of thought or being, and their implicit marriages, is a psychological continuum, important elements of which have yet to be identified. Psychologically considered, the *Songs* include their own act of union.)

Though it is the readings that will show the limits of value of this view of the *Songs,* I believe the accidents of my own mental life which brought me to the view may have their interest too. Such attempts at revelation have their own limits and dangers, of course. But my reader may judge. What follows is a highly schematized history of my response to Blake's work, especially the *Songs.*

At the heart of my feelings about Blake's poetry is a sense for his frequent presentation of minds utterly exposed to experience—bare, sensitized minds, highly vulnerable to the people and things around them, and yet somehow not aware of what they endure. At the same time, I am also affected by a sense of Blake's power to imply or show that the uncompromised regard of this exposure to pain is possible, even necessary. (His way of treasuring vulnerable characters, often ignorant of their own psychological state, is to regard them steadily.) Though all poets make deep life stand still, no poet reaches deeper into life or arrests it more significantly for our scrutiny.

Closely allied is my strong sense that Blake's metaphors very often turn on the idea of death. It is the subject on which he draws to identify the basis of human vulnerability. In Blake's world it is death that limits us to mortality, death that requires us to accommodate ourselves to the natural world or perish, death that defines the natural world in which we live. When I first read the *Songs,* I had just been exposed to the risk of death in war for some months, and though I had no doubt that Blake understood death's ubiquitous presence in many disguises—the garden of love is filled with graves; chimney sweepers are locked in black coffins; the Raven of death nests in the man-made tree of holy Mystery; the cycle of life in London begins in the marriage Hearse; man and fly are married in death; the Little Black Boy anticipates deliverance from social prejudice by leaving forever his unalterable black body; some nameless power dared to clasp the Tyger's deadly terrors—I thought I might be overreading its force for him. But as time passed, several strands of evidence served to reinforce rather than to diminish my first powerful impression.

At Thel's grave plot, the vision of life as hostile and deadly seemed to me like much of Blake's poetry, from the *Songs* through the prophecies, to combine human vulnerability and the steady regard of threatening forces. Though the two functions are often divided, so that, for example, "London's" young Harlot is vulnerable, while "London's" speaker (in some sense vulnerable himself) looks steadily at her vulnerability, Thel experiences both functions in full measure. True, she is enabled by her creator, Blake, to flee the world in which death figures prominently, but until she does, she sees death everywhere, and it promises to define the life she contemplates. Neither blaming Thel for giving up the chance for a life of natural experience nor congratulating her for turning away very sensibly from a bad scene seemed to me a reasonable way of handling her vision of things. Blake's treatment of death, viewed with an eye to her psychology, left me feeling that there was no simple resolution of the dilemma the poem represents. It also made me think of Blake's Self-examination and Self-annihilation, and of his Jesus, whose sacrificial death sets us free and yet leaves each of us struggling individually for redemption, and of Albion's repeated dying in *Jerusalem.* Obviously much in Blake's work turned on death and the perceptions of life it begets and on death and our ways of responding to it imaginatively. These conclusions were not new in Blake studies, but they seemed to me to occupy a place of much greater significance than the amount of time spent on them in the criticism implies they might have.

The very first sentences of David Erdman's Preface to the *Blake Concordance* gave a certain palpable support to my view that the poet's interest in death was marked, and they also offered presumptive evidence for my belief that Blake's readers make less of the fact than they might reasonably do. Erdman begins:

> Each new concordance brings its particular surprises, those most immediately accessible being some of the words that come out at the top of the frequency count—or at the bottom. We may have expected to find MAN, LOVE, ETERNAL, and EARTH among Blake's most used words, but not DEATH so near the top or NIGHT so far ahead of DAY.[4]

In fact, the only words that occur more frequently than "death" in the poetry are "all," "O," "upon," "Los," "like," "as," "Albion," and "man." In short, the only words that might be reckoned words of substance ahead of "death" in frequency are "all," "Los," "Albion," and "man," and two of them are proper nouns. But how he uses the word (and those closely related to it) is the important thing. A psychologist perhaps unique in the combination of his great sensitivity and great detachment, Blake almost never uses it to refer to physical death. Without morbidity, he associates "death," "dead," and their proxies with the fallen world that imposes itself on us— the world through which we move as we live our lives, stumbling "all night over bones of the dead."[5] They help to characterize our natural and our social context. Or he uses them to suggest a sense of ourselves or a point of view we have adopted, often unconsciously, as a result of being imposed upon by the world of death around us: "They clothed me in the clothes of death." One way or another, Blake lets us know that death does not simply mark the human terminus we cannot avoid, the time and place of our dissolution, though it is precisely the fear that it may do so, he understands, that gives death its power over us. Aware that we are unconsciously intimidated by it, he treats death dynamically, as a conditioning force variously disguised in the world around us, and as a force we incorporate into our unconscious life as we accommodate ourselves to the threats it poses in natural life, in order that we may survive.

I knew Blake was not alone in his sensitivity to death as a proximate force in our daily lives. Many of his predecessors for a hundred and fifty years or more before the publication of the *Songs* had left evidence of their preoccupation with the subject, which roughly parallels the emergence of highly individualized Protestant sects and the philosophical regard of the New Science. This long-lived and complicated interest in death may be said to have been brought to resolution in a not entirely satisfactory way with the posthumous publication of Hume's *Essays on Suicide, and the Immortality of the Soul* in 1783.[6] There Hume argues that we have only that control over life and death represented by our power to do away with ourselves, a power he believes we have every right to exercise. But he discounts the possibility of an afterlife, as if to settle the disturbing matter once and for all. Most others who wrote on the subject were either personally moved to reveal their sense of loneliness and uncertainity in the face of death—John Donne, Jonathan Swift, Samuel Johnson, and hundreds more.[7] Or they sought to control death by incorporating it into a system of things that reduced its power to harass the imagination. Often, existing religious systems that had grown powerless to help the anxiety of doubt were modified to accomplish this reduction of death's disturbing presence. Or entirely secular activities, from the institution of charity hospitals and soup kitchens to the resuscitation of the apparently dead by scientific means, were undertaken to hold death back.[8]

It seemed apparent that despite Blake's interest in social reform and his invention of a psycho-Christianity (both were hallmarks of the response to death among his predecessors and contemporaries), he was decidely un-like the others. Certainly he shared with them an inescapable heritage. Protestant man, though not every Protestant, by the logic of his religious position, might very well suppose himself individually responsible for arranging the terms of his own covenant with God—a lonely job, full of doubt. And the heirs of the New Science, unless they had religious faith, found themselves without the sure means of appraising the nature of their relationship to the physical universe they occupied. It seemed to operate in accordance with immutable mechanistic laws requiring neither God nor man for their continuance, a world of dead ratios without human meaning. Without meaning, life is uncertainty, anxiety, the threat of nonentity, death. It was in this context that Cambridge Platonism, Christian mortalism,[9] and Humean skepticism were formulated, along with many other religious and secular structures, the net effect of each being to reduce death's power to give pain. Sensitive and introspective as he was, Blake could no more have escaped this heritage than he could have chosen to be born in a different age, or, like Thel, chosen to remove himself from the grave plot to a different place, where there was no death. But instead of locating death reductively in a new or resurrected system, or, like Hume, naturalizing the idea of death by relentlessly identifying human limitations, Blake made its effects on our mental life the chief object of his regard. As sensitive as Thel to death's disguised presences, he was also able to do what she could only avoid—to look at it steadily, without loss of sensitivity and without loss of detachment.

It was with this reinforced sense that death is indeed a very important subject for Blake, and that he treats it not morbidly but as a conditioning force in the world around us and as a force we incorporate so that it defines us no less than the world in which we live, that I have interpreted the *Songs* in the present study. Instead of representing death primarily as the frightening power that dissolves life, Blake sees its functions and transformations at work in the minds of his characters. Death becomes the variably disguised object of his scrutiny, out of which he generates a psychology of redemption. But in keeping with the dynamic power of death and the range of meanings it may imply, Blake's redemption is not a system one may adopt "philosophically." It is rather a process one may try to make a part of one's imaginative life, a process that makes use of a disciplined introspection, working at often hidden feelings.

(I will be reading the *Songs* with three ideas in mind. For the moment, it will be useful to anticipate these ideas in isolation. First, as I have stressed now in various ways, Blake often talks about both the natural and the human-made worlds in the terms of death and its hold on the imagination. Second, Blake may be said to prefer over his other characters those who have come to understand that death fills the world in many shapes (as social evil, as formal religion, as parents' education of children), who are sensitive enough to see that in their earlier lives they have been coerced by its threatening presences, and who are brave (detached) enough to survive the emotional consequences to themselves of such disturbing recognitions. And third, taken as a whole, *Songs of Innocence and of Experience* is primarily a record of the coercion of mental life, covering both the psychological consequences of such coercion and the possibility of getting past it)

It would be hard to overemphasize the seriousness and intensity of Blake's concern, directly expressed in "To Tirzah," that all of us have been conditioned by a threatening environment or by one of its representatives; we have been "moulded" by the Mother of our "Mortal Part," so that our "Nostrils Eyes & Ears" are bound, our senses and our beings limited. The threatening world around us determines what we see, what we feel, and what we become, a mere function of mortality's requirements for survival; but we scarcely know at all that it is so. If we did, there would be no moments of discovery of the sort we find in the speaker's obviously new recognition of his mortal mother's hold on him in "To Tirzah." We do not know that we yield to coercion, necessarily yield, it turns out, and yet yield at great cost. And we are not in a position to know what we become as a result of our unconscious yielding, nor by what process we have been made what we are.

It is this threatening aspect of our earthly predicament that Thel identifies in her vision of the grave. Blake's poetry argues as if we are all controlled unconsciously by such a view of things, unless we can somehow discover our confinement of vision and accept the conscious threat of death such recognition includes. Imagine that Thel had accommodated herself to her own vision of the grave by rationalizing its deadly qualities into something more benign, that she had learned to live in that falsely benign context and had *become* what she had learned. What would it take for her to change? As it is, Thel escapes the threatening predicament by refusing to join life. Like the speaker of "To Tirzah," the rest of us have no such option. To survive in the world Thel sees, which is the world we see, our minds distort the terrible truth to make it bearable, as Blake implies in several of the *Songs.* Here it may be enough to point out that the emblem of humanity's need to rationalize its predicament is that shortly after the Fall "Mercy changed Death into Sleep." Death threatens, and to flee its presence nonphysically (we do not have Thel's choice, after all) our minds distort its grim reality into something we can bear. As a result, we see with blinders on, and we become what we behold. The life-preserving mechanism paradoxically reduces life.

It is generally acknowledged that very few of the *Songs of Innocence* present characters unaffected by physical and emotional dangers in the natural world.[10] The child in the "Introduction" and in "The Lamb" are among the few persons in these poems to feel an unqualified sense of union with the world around them. They are in the blessed state in which people and forces outside them seem "continuous" with, not inimical to, themselves, as Robert F. Gleckner, John Holloway, David Erdman, and others have in different ways shown.[11] On a cloud, the child of the "Introduction" expresses a series of unself-conscious commands that are obeyed, the result being the Piper's songs that are presumably to unite all children in joy. And the child-speaker of "The Lamb" is seen to be "identical" with the lamb and with Christ—"I a child & thou a lamb, / We are called by [Christ's] name." It is worth observing that in these poems, when a wish is immediately fulfilled, the wisher feels the continuity of events outside him with himself; what is inside his mind is given shape in his environment, which for the occasion, at least, appears absolutely congenial. Similarly, when one observes others with whom one feels identical, the world of persons besides oneself appears entirely congenial. "Laughing Song," like the "Introduction" and "The Lamb," celebrates this affinity of inside with outside and of one with another. There, laughter and song are one; so are the children and the speaker; and so are the human voices and the voices of woods, stream, air, hill, meadow, and grasshopper.

Understood from the children's point of view, and not from Blake's or the Piper's or our own, Innocence is a condition of unself-conscious indentification with the world and the people outside one.[12] Such unself-consciousness might be defined negatively as a failure on the part of the child to perceive inimical elements in the world. It has seen nothing that requires it to protect the organism that is itself, and so it has no sense of itself as a separate entity. Quite the contrary, it feels or thinks in terms of its continuity with persons, objects, and events around it. Few readers, of course, can join this world of unity, even when invited to do so by an unself-conscious speaker who lives there, as is the case in "Laughing Song": "Come live & be merry and join with me, / To sing the sweet chorus of Ha, Ha, He." Self-consciousness, or the knowledge that the world is not a unity, restrains us in some degree from membership in joy's coherence. And this restraint may be said to represent part of the meaning of the poem. But we may also be able to imagine the unity, even recollect its qualities, by the exercise of selective memory from our own pasts. Certainly we can do more than simply distinguish the children of unity from ourselves; we can appreciate something of the nature of their way of seeing and being. We can both be "ourselves" and in some sense be them. Awareness of this capacity is important for an understanding of the *Songs*.

What about the other *Songs of Innocence?* Do they not, as various critics observe, register a world of sorrow and disillusion? The answer depends on whose point of view one takes. The reader may see in them a world of sorrow. Obviously the Chimney Sweeper and the Little Black Boy are both children driven very hard by a cruel society. Or Blake the man may be thought of as using irony in order to express his anger at society's treat-ment of the boys. The last line of "The Little Black Boy" and the last of "The Chimney Sweeper" both undercut the palliating vision earlier presented by the child of the poem. "So if all do their duty, they need not fear harm" may of course be read as Blake's ironic way of rendering illusory the comfort of Tom Dacre's dream. "And be like him and he will then love me" may be Blake's ironic way of rendering illusory the comfort of the Black mother's lesson; if the Black Boy would rather be loved by the white than to accept his mother's view of him as especially benefited by experience, what good is her lesson, after all? But for the moment consider these *Songs of Innocence* from the point of view of the children who experience their action rather than from the point of view of the reader or Blake. It is the children, finally, who dwell in Innocence or leave that state, and not we or Blake. It is their point of view, in and out of Innocence, that provides a means of understanding their psychology. Let us assume both the Chimney Sweeper and the Little Black Boy to be consistent in their attitudes from first to last. The reader then would have to conclude that "So if all do their duty, they need not fear harm" was literally intended by the speaker. And it would follow that he was taken in by Tom Dacre's dream. That is, one would understand that the speaker accepts the rationalization the dream amounts to, masking and transforming as it does the deadly social present of the chimney sweepers with a promise of heavenly protection. A full reading offered later will provide more evidence for this way of looking at the poem.

Read with the same expectations for consistency, the Little Black Boy's "And be like him and he will then love me" underscores a similar presentation of social evil and the speaker's psychological escape from that evil. What is most important about the last line of "The Little Black Boy" is that it permits the reader to see the mind of the child working at two levels, quite self-deceivingly. At one level the boy accepts his mother's lesson so thoroughly that he recounts the occasion of its delivery to him with unself-conscious pleasure—"She took me on her lap and kissed me"—and then he repeats the lesson verbatim, surely an act of faith in its efficacy. But at another level, it turns out, he makes it something very different from what it claims to be, namely, the promise of a future state in which his spiritual superiority (which his mother tries to get him to realize he enjoys in the *present* life) will enable him to help the English boy. Instead, he finds in it a reason for believing he can become enough like the white boy for the white boy to love him. In effect, the Black Boy has both accepted his mother's lesson and repudiated it, by using it, inappropriately, to cope with the problem it was intended to transcend.[13]

(If the children of other *Songs of Innocence* are similarly moved to rationalize their early recognitions of danger to themselves, their first apprehensions of mortality, then it may be appropriate to redefine Innocence so that it includes, in addition to the child's sense of unself-conscious identification with the world and the people outside him, his unself-conscious will to prolong that sense in the face of evidence that might be expected to displace it. It is precisely the weight of such evidence that has encouraged readers to see disillusion in *Songs of Innocence,* or to see Blake's irony working to undercut the children's improbable willingness to maintain their faith, though that willingness seems not to have been well identified or understood. But the weight of evidence ought not to obscure the fact that these children *know not what they do.* Read with the child's point of view in mind, the poems reveal two crucial facts about the departure from Innocence. First, it is a departure reluctantly undertaken, and second, the forces initiating that departure seem to precipitate unconscious mental operations, ultimately self-deceiving or defensive in nature.

All of the other *Songs of Innocence* do not as explicitly support the thesis I have proposed as do the two I have so far considered. But the others fall readily into one of the two categories I have identified, or they include elements of both in a special equilibrium. That is, they present characters who feel unself-consciously united with the world, or characters who unself-consciously prolong that feeling in the face of adverse evidence, or they join the two. Along with the "Introduction," "The Lamb," and "Laughing Song," the first group includes "The Shepherd," "Spring," and "Infant Joy." In addition to "The Little Black Boy" and "The Chimney Sweeper," the second includes "A Cradle Song," "Night," "A Dream," "The Little Boy Lost" and "The Little Boy Found" considered as a unified pair, and "On Anothers Sorrow." "The Ecchoing Green" and "Nurses Song," both of which include grown-ups sympathetic to innocents who feel unself-consciously at home in the world, but grown-ups who do not unself-consciously share the innocents' vision, provide a psychological bridge to the third group, in which a firm and realistic adult view seems to correct the vision of congenial innocence or to admonish adults who may misunderstand that innocence—"The Blossom," "Holy Thursday," and "The Divine Image."

These three last-named poems are themselves a bridge to *Songs of Experience,* which present characters who of their own accord address or who are made to address the forces of death in the world outside them. Self-conscious of danger, or somehow urged or otherwise moved to become conscious of it, they confront their trouble or they feel the pain of it. If they try to rationalize or otherwise dispose of their difficulties, as in different ways Ona and the Sick Rose seem to do, they are brought up short by editorial indictment or in a confrontation with another character, so that, unlike the Little Black Boy or The Chimney Sweeper of Innocence, no comfort is available to them. Psychologically the "obverse" of his counterpart in Innocence, the Chimney Sweeper of Experience knows he has been

imposed upon, and he resents it: "because I am happy, & dance & sing, /
They think they have done me no injury." His words make it clear that he has
an unvarnished view of his own predicament, but they also reveal that he has
begun to appraise the mental operations of his mother and father, who, as he
sees it, are able to believe, somehow, that they have done him no harm,
when of course they have "clothed [him] in the clothes of death." And
beyond that knowledge, he shows a further psychological sophistication by
associating his parents with other creators of a false heaven: "God & his
Priest & King / Who make up a heaven of our misery." Though the Sweeper's
association has social and religious levels of meaning, I wish here to stress
only the acute psychological consciousness with which it shows this child of
Experience to be endowed. Unlike the Chimney Sweeper of Innocence, he
is fooled neither by himself nor by others, at one level of consciousness, at
least. Somehow he has begun to see things "for what they are." What he sees
is only a beginning, of course, but it marks a crucial difference between the
children of Innocence and of Experience.

Among the other characters in *Songs of Experience* who see into their
manipulation by persons, ideas, and institutions that make up their world,
or who see into the manipulation of others, are the Little Vagabond, the
School Boy, Lyca, and the speakers of "The Clod & the Pebble," "Holy
Thursday," "The Little Girl Lost," "The Little Girl Found," "The Sick Rose,"
"The Angel," "My Pretty Rose Tree," "Ah! Sun-Flower," "The Garden of
Love," "London," "The Human Abstract," "A Poison Tree," "A Little Girl
Lost," "A Little Boy Lost," and "To Tirzah." In fact, the discovery of destruc-
tive psychological coercion to oneself is the chief subject of *Songs of
Experience,* though needless to say the subject has many facets and grada-
tions. It brings some of the characters in the poems to the threshold of
control over their own lives through a new consciousness of their predica-
ment, or it reveals through the speakers' observations to the reader the
heavy failure of such visionary control.

As close readings of the *Songs* in the following chapters will make clear,
the roots of psychological coercion run deep. For example, the parents
who join God, Priest, and King in delivering their own son to the deadly
life of a chimney sweeper, along with Ona's and Lyca's parents and with
Tirzah, are themselves unconscious agents of institutions and attitudes
long since invented to protect life against dangers that life fears without
understanding. It would be simple indeed to think that Ona's complex
guilt, related as it is in a dozen ways to the expectations for civilized living
buried in the mind of a whole society, could be remedied by an enlight-

ened father. Though it is true that things might have been better at home for Ona—Lyca's parents are "better" in the matter of coercive conditioning, it seems; Tirzah is worse—no simple solution is available for her, any more than for her father, who is a product, with his daughter, of the same deadly heritage. His mother was a Tirzah of some sort, too.

Other *Songs of Experience,* by their very subject and tone, imply both a complexity of cautionary restraint in the mind's contours and the mind's occasional releases from such complexity. "The Fly," for all its mischievous paradox, raises clear questions about the uncertainties of the borderline between one being and another, and between one's own species of being and another. The speaker's recognition is not that he has been painfully imposed upon by another person or by some institutional system of things but that his conditioned sense of himself as "finite" and "identifiable" has been put into doubt or nullified. Here he is, and there is the fly, and then suddenly *he* is the fly, or at least he can no longer see a real difference between the fly and himself. Though this self-reflexive behavior may not be referred to the speaker's recognition and overthrow of coercive conditioning, it does mark the overthrow of his conventionally induced perception. He has experienced a minor vision of the truth of things beyond himself and yet including him. For reasons one can only guess at, he treats the vision comically. Similar and yet more portentous for self-discovery is the experience of "The Tyger's" speaker, whose vision results in his redefinition of God the Creator, and of his relationship with Him, the lamb, the Tyger, and with himself as well. Among the realizations thrust upon him is this one: that quite beyond what man may do to man, there are natural forces of destruction woven into the very fabric of the physical universe. These forces also need psychological management by those who want to be saved.

A few characters in *Songs of Experience,* far from being on the verge of some productive discovery about themselves or in the midst of discovery, seemed closed off from such a blessing altogether. The Nurse and the Sick Rose are two of these. Their presence in *Songs of Experience* reinforces the idea and the value of Self-examination nevertheless, for both of them are identified dramatically as psychologically wanting. The Nurse, contrasted with the Nurse of Innocence, identifies herself not only as confining in her treatment of the children who are her charges but as defeated in her view of life and of herself. She uses the knowledge that her adulthood is spent in "disguise"—that is, controlled by suppressed desire, which she seems to have no real means of handling—not as the beginning of Self-examination

but as a general indictment of life and as a threat about their own adult-
hoods to the children. The Sick Rose is treated by the speaker as if it were a
clinical case in need of diagnosis. Whatever its state may be, the Rose
seems incapable of understanding and commenting on its own predica-
ment. The most passive of Blake's characters in Experience (even the Sun-
flower and the Clod have a point of view), the Sick Rose endures defeat
through an incapacity to engage life reciprocally. For the moment it will be
enough to say that both of these characters, Nurse and Sick Rose, face
serious unpleasantness, but unlike those on hard times in Innocence, they
do not promote a happy delusion about their bad predicaments, and un-
like most characters in Experience, their speech or other responsive behav-
ior implies no constructive course of action. Their pasts control them.
Indeed, they are their pasts.

It may be important to ask whether the voices of speakers, which I have
understood to represent "characters," are not after all disembodied, so that
I have invented an implausible critical fiction. I think the answer to the
question is not to be found in a completely characterized mind available
through any single voice in the *Songs*—no such completeness obtains. Nor
is it to be found in a simple compositing of all the voices to build the "one
mind" of the *Songs*. The voices vary enormously in emotional strength,
intelligence, sensitivity, and temperament. But they all collect to suggest a
continuing mental process, which, if not complete, is certainly full. It
seems reasonable, finally, to think of the voices as speaking for characters,
because so viewed, they contribute to a full sense of Blake's vision of the
human predicament. And its representation, dynamic as it is, invites us as
much to participate in the process it identifies as to consider it analytically.

Innocence and Experience, as I have so far treated them, imply a transi-
tion between the one and the other, during which the reluctance to ac-
knowledge threats to life in Innocence (The Chimney Sweeper's rational-
ization, for example) gives way to the willingness to admit that something
is very wrong, and perhaps to indict and correct the trouble. In fact, the
Songs may be thought of as representing a continuous psychological pro-
cess, an inevitable movement from the state of Innocence, in which (from
the child's point of view) one enjoys an unself-conscious unity with one's
surroundings, to an encounter with evidence that threatens life, such evi-
dence being for a time displaced by rationalization, but later intruding into
the conscious mind. At this point the mind may be thought of as in Experi-
ence by virtue of its inability to rationalize the threatening evidence (the
Nurse), or a distinctly different matter, by virtue of its willingness to accept

it (the second Chimney Sweeper). Where the mind can no longer rational-
ize the evidence and yet cannot deal with the problem it represents, the
evidence is likely to register as fear, pain, or the sense of defeat. Where the
mind receives the evidence with knowledge enough to give it "meaning,"
the evidence becomes a problem that is understood to need a solution or a
problem for which a solution is sought and sometimes found. For exam-
ple, the speaker of "To Tirzah" believes he can explain the reasons for his
circumscribed perception and the way to escape domination by his
mother.

As I have already indicated, one ought probably to avoid expecting the
"mind" of the foregoing model to reveal itself throughout the poems as a
single human psychology or as consistently intelligent or consistently sensi-
tive. Lyca seems to be healthy, whereas the Sick Rose is not; the speaker of
"The Fly" is a metaphysician who makes and breaks analogies, whereas
Ona seems hardly to know the most obvious implications of her actions;
the speaker of "The Tyger" is struck deep by an aspect of creation, whereas
the Sun-flower is weary of time. Individual though they are, these charac-
ters help to illuminate the psychological process that is the movement
from Innocence through Experience, control of which is ultimately re-
quired by Blake's Self-annihilation, his remedy for death in the world and
for the vision it generates. The alternative to such emotional "dying" into
new life is to survive behind a wall of self-delusion, narrowly defined by
the very threats to life one refuses unconsciously to acknowledge and to
assimilate.

In the *Songs,* Blake tells us a good deal about the formation of the vision
of death, the Selfhood that needs annihilation. Unless this accumulation of
largely unconscious experience is recognized in some detail, the process
of redemption—one's liberation from that accumulation—is likely to be
understood more as an idea than as a deeply felt realization. It seems
obviously in the spirit of Blake's way of writing and thinking to prefer the
second to the first. The following chapter is based on this assumption. But
before beginning it, I should like to say one more word about redemption
here, a point reinforced, I believe, by much of what follows.

Blake's insistent treatment of redemption throughout his work results in
the close reader's increasing sense of enrichment and complexity. But
certain difficulties stand in the way of our appreciating this accretion. In
the *Songs of Innocence and of Experience* the psychology of redemption is
detailed. Yet, as I have said, no single mind is a vehicle for its entire display.
We see bits and pieces of the process implied by a wide range of quite

different kinds of characters in various predicaments, though of course the broad outlines of the process are implied by the psychological principle distinguishing (and uniting) the two sets of *Songs*. In the major prophecies, single characters do in fact annihilate the Selfhood, but it is not easy to infer in very full detail the psychology that sponsors the redemption. Certainly more evidence is given to us there than we can handle critically. At times the Self-annihilation seems an act of individual will and at times a gift of grace.[14] In one sense these redemptions are individual; in another, universal. They may be understood to take place over great stretches of time and space, and yet they may be accomplished very locally, in a single pulsation of the artery. And finally, Blake's practical expectations for himself and others who attempt such redemption seem complicated. To leave off is to die; on the other hand, it seems there is no completing the process. According to Henry Crabb Robinson, Blake said as late as February 1826, "Every man has a Devil in himself, and the conflict between his *Self* and God is perpetually going on."[15] Blake also tells us in the late Inscription in the Autograph Album of William Upcott (1826) that he was "Born 28 Novr 1757 in London and has died several times since."[16] Apparently he realized in looking at himself that no complete annihilation of the Selfhood is possible. The mind is far too complicated for one to search deep enough into its dark pits and turns, or always to hold on to the burst or flicker of new vision one may experience there. Perhaps no consciousness is so penetrant as to keep the mind from protecting itself from more life than it can bear.[17] Though these and other complications in Blake's redemptive world are unlikely to be reduced to easy symmetries, some of them, at least, may be clarified by enlargement.

2

Selfhood's Making

Ideas closely related to "Selfhood" have a well-advertised place in forms of Buddhism, Gnosticism, and Christianity.[1] "Self-examination" also represents a widely identified range of ideas, Montaigne's "je suis moy-mesmes la matiere de mon livre"[2] being only the first modern expression of a truth St. Augustine might also have spoken with accuracy about his *Confessions*. More to the point, twentieth-century psychologists—Freud, Jung, Hubbard, for instance—have made the close regard of one's inner life an ordinary matter. And the belief that Self-annihilation, or something akin to a willing sacrificial death, literal or not, is the act that precedes rebirth has been made familiar by James George Frazer, Arnold van Gennep, W. K. C. Guthrie, and many besides.[3] Whether we know all these sources, and maybe others as well, or only some, the ideas that fall under Blake's terms are so widely available as to obscure the possibility that his views about Selfhood and its annihilation can be experienced and understood keenly, as something unique, however like other views they may be.

In the first chapter I tried to show that Blake displays the mind as "continuous" with the world it occupies (Innocence) and, later, the mind coerced by that world and yet unwilling to acknowledge to itself the damage of coercion (self-deceiving Innocence). I also tried to show that he represents the mind at a later stage as coerced and overpowered by the coercion, or coerced and quite able to identify the coercion and to object to it (Experience). It is in a way obvious that in addition to giving us clues about these general responses, Blake gives us others about the radical nature of individually received experiences. He states or implies what it is that affects the mind deeply (typically pain[4] and not pleasure in the *Songs*) and what in the way of a developing sense of self, or Selfhood, results from the engagement. As I have already suggested, this Selfhood, probably constructed on a birthright of "selfishness," as Frye indicates,[5] routinely converts painful experience into something less threatening than in fact it is ("rationalization") or displaces it from consciousness ("repression"), and in the process of doing so enlarges Selfhood's domain.

These two mechanisms of Selfhood are so complicated that the only satisfactory way of understanding how Blake treated them is to observe them in operation in a poem. Nevertheless, a word or two about them may be useful in advance. It seems clear that repression always accompanies the process of rationalization. It may not be possible to say how much the Little Black Boy displaces his pain from consciousness altogether (repression) and how much he makes its root cause acceptable to consciousness by means of imagining good times in heaven (rationalization), but clearly he does some of both. On the other hand, repression may control a mind to the exclusion or near exclusion of rationalization, in which case the character—the being—so dominated ceases to function in the workaday world. The Sick Rose, I shall argue, represses painful experience much more than she rationalizes it. In fact, she may not be able to rationalize it at all.

One may imagine a Blakean ideal in which painful experience is accepted for "what it is," without repression or rationalization. One may further imagine a hierarchy representing psychological movement for the worse, away from the ideal, as follows: (1) seeing a painful thing for "what it is," (2) rationalizing a painful experience, (3) repressing a painful experience. Though rationalization does some of the work of repression, it continues to make the painful content available to consciousness in a disguised form. Repression, on the other hand, denies the painful content altogether. Rationalization implies dealing with the world in "false" terms. Unmitigated repression implies withdrawal from the world, at least with reference to the potential activity represented by the repressed material. The hierarchy I have adduced is artificial, of course, because the categories it identifies are fluid in the reality of mental dynamics, but useful nevertheless, I believe. In the three readings that follow, readings of "The Chimney Sweeper" of Innocence, *The Book of Thel,* and "The Lilly," we shall encounter characters who repress pain (the Chimney Sweeper), rationalize it (the

Chimney Sweeper), or confront it "as it is" (Thel and Lilly). How they behave in the face of coercive experience helps us to understand something about how Selfhood is formed and how it operates.

Though the Chimney Sweeper identifies his mother's death as something he "knows" in the very first words he speaks, he treats the loss in such a way as to make it clear that it is too potent emotionally for him to handle, either directly or in the terms of rationalization, which would at least make it available to consciousness in a verbally disguised form.[6] What he does instead is to move swiftly from his mother's death to that other cruel fact of his young life, his father's selling him. His statement in the remainder of the song is an elaborate rationalization that makes a proxy father available to him. But he neither mentions his mother again nor builds a rationalization that makes her (or a version of her) a part of his fantasy life. He may be said to have put away from consciousness the most painful experience of his brief existence and to have rationalized his present life in metaphors deriving from a pain he can in some degree manage, that associated with the loss of his father. This removal of mother from consciousness, even in a verbally disguised form, after her emotional domination of the first three lines of the poem, should not be taken to signify that her death has no continuing effect on his emotional life, only that he must turn away from it as more than he can bear. It may be supposed that at the foundation of his unique Selfhood is this loss, which he cannot cope with verbally in anything like an immediately derivative way. Nevertheless the rationalized correction of his universe, through the agency of the restored and greatly improved father who sold him, is so comprehensive as to overcome not only the loss of his earthly father but the loss of his mother as well. For the correction includes life everlasting in God the Father's heaven.

In the first three lines of the poem, which begin with the single reference to his mother's death, the Chimney Sweeper reveals his extreme vulnerability as a consequence of his loss: "When my mother died I was very young, / And my father sold me while yet my tongue, / Could scarcely cry weep weep weep weep." He has received two blows that deprive him of his sense of connection with the world. His mother (his love) is dead. His father (his protector) has become the child's seller, and he has acted in this cruel way in some sense "because" the mother died. Cut off radically from the life he knew, the Chimney Sweeper is left to make what he can of his predicament. One may understand that important elements of his Selfhood were abruptly wounded into being, leaving him to reinvent a relationship with the world around him, and to reinvent it in terms that his suffering mind will allow.

Closely allied to the child's sense of loss, and intensifying it, is his age: "my father sold me while yet my tongue / Could scarcely cry weep weep weep weep." The repeated word, as has often been observed, suggests both "sweep," as it might be spoken by one too young to have mastered it, and "weep."[7] This repetition is at one level a sign of imaginative fixity. It implies the Chimney Sweeper's psychological concentration on the painful elements clustered in the first three lines. Fixed, his mind is unable to carry the narrative forward. On the verge of unmastered emotion, however, he moves through a complex transition between the third and fourth lines, and he emerges with an apparently firm grip on himself: "So your chimneys I sweep & in soot I sleep." Though the whole tone of expression has changed, this line follows the three preceding in accordance with a simple logic something like this: I sweep your chimneys (and sleep in soot) because my mother died when I was young, leaving me to my father, who sold me. But the psychological distance between the third and fourth lines is too great to be explained by this logic alone. The speaker does indeed have a grip on himself. But the new control is hardly a sign that he understands and accepts his real predicament. A look backward in the poem suggests that it cannot be; the lines there, which so painfully recollect his mother and his father, culminate in the pathetically repeated "weep." Even the possible pleasure of self-pity, which might be a part of his recollection, could not efface his deep sense of loss and abandonment. And a look forward seems to confirm the view. There, and for the remainder of the poem, the Chimney Sweeper is involved in a relationship with Tom Dacre that provides both boys with a falsely grounded comfort of their own devising.

The apparently crisp summing up of present reality in the fourth line, then, invites the speculation that at some level it means something different from what it says literally. It may be regarded as a swiftly wrought evasion of painful feelings, given logical form, but not at all well understood by the boy. It also sounds like a burst of resentment directed against the whole world, though nominally against those who like the boy's father are involved in the exploitation of chimney sweepers: "So your chimneys I sweep & in soot I sleep." There is something accusatory in the statement, which in fact helps him to get past his pain, for an instant at least. Finally, the fourth line is the transition from his painful past, which at one level or another dominates his present, to the world in which he lives with Tom.

He has moved from the world of his mother's death, which he cannot manage, to the world of unprotected chimney sweepers, which he can control in consciousness, however specious the currency he uses.

The remaining five stanzas of the poem reveal many of the consequences of the Chimney Sweeper's past in his present. These include the characteristics of the existence into which he has been sold, the nature of his relationship with Tom, and the ways in which his mind works. The three categories are overlapping, so that to start with the second, the relationship with Tom, as the speaker does, is quickly to get to the other two.

> There's little Tom Dacre, who cried when his head
> That curl'd like a lambs back, was shav'd, so I said.
> Hush Tom never mind it, for when your head's bare,
> You know that the soot cannot spoil your white hair.

The first words of the stanza both introduce a new subject, the friendship with Tom, and continue the old one, unprotected, cruelly treated little boys who cry. No sooner has the speaker stopped himself from weeping than we find Tom weeping too. This tenacity of his special pain, its power to survive and reappear in a disguised form in the mind of the little autobiographer, right after he had put a lid on it with his understandably resentful "So your chimneys I sweep . . . " implies that it is to continue to figure prominently in the poem, or seen from another point of view, to figure prominently in his life. The continuation of interest in forlorn boys who weep, from the third line to the fifth, besides supporting the view that the fourth line masks but does not control the emotionally potent material in the preceding three, also suggests that the Chimney Sweeper identifies himself with Tom. Given their circumstances, the identification is hardly surprising. But its selectivity and its intensity are surprising.

Both boys are sacrificed to the purposes of their employment, and one may assume both have been sold and shorn. Both work and sleep in soot, both are lonely and sad, both are in want of a loving parent. But the Chimney Sweeper does not find his sole comfort in this congruence, as one might who felt that misery was reduced by company. Instead, he uses it as a context in which to make a new structure for explaining their lives. His words of comfort are the instrument of this deliverance, offered right after his friend's head "That curl'd like a lambs back, was shav'd":

> Hush Tom never mind it, for when your head's bare,
> You know that the soot cannot spoil your white hair.

This rationalization, pathetic or even absurd as it might be in another context, pacifies Tom: "And so he was quiet. . . ." It also anticipates all the important elements of Tom's dream, which is to become the structure they use to explain their lives. Like the speaker's helpful support, the dream includes a comforting presence that moves an apparent victim from darkness to salvation. All of the sweepers in the dream, "lock'd up in coffins of black," are freed by an Angel, after which they wash themselves. Then "naked & white," they rise. Tom's white hair is saved from soot by the speaker's words, and the sweeps' bodies are made white after release from black coffins by the Angel's key. Just as the speaker's words of comfort to Tom foreshadow the dream, so the end of the dream, in which Tom is assured by the Angel that if he is good, God will be his father, foreshadows the end of the poem. There the speaker generalizes the hopeful message of the dream in a final expression of unconsciously arranged mutuality between Tom and himself and between the dream and their external world: "So if all do their duty, they need not fear harm."

The movement of the poem from first to last is the speaker's psychological management of the problem he identifies starkly, and unconsciously turns away from in stanza one. Unable to face it directly, he tries by projection to deal with it through Tom, whose predicament is his own. Needing comfort in his loneliness and near despair, he gives Tom fatherly comfort, and in so doing, comforts himself; and with his words of comfort, he engenders in Tom, or imagines he engenders, a dream, which he recounts with a command of detail so fresh and compelling to him that he shifts from the past tense to the present:

> And by came an Angel who had a bright key,
> And he open'd the coffins & set them all free.
> Then down a green plain leaping laughing they run
> And wash in a river and shine in the Sun.
>
> Then naked & white, all their bags left behind,
> They rise upon clouds, and sport in the wind.

The shift in tense makes the action of the dream more immediate, its availability to him greater. In fact, he has appropriated it after having supplied its contours in embryo.[8] The appropriation is a fitting prelude to the Chimney Sweeper's accepting the words of assurance to Tom. The Sweeper begets the dream, he appropriates it, and he accepts its final message—that if he is good, God will be his father. The offer of paternity is conditional, of course. It requires him to work at the trade his actual father sold him into. But he is prepared for the job by reason of his ability to avoid seeing it for what it is. The ability is very complexly wrought, and it is pitiable.[9]

W. J. T. Mitchell seems to me right in saying almost every Blake poem is "a perfectly adequate, self-sustaining text which does not need the accompanying illustrations to make it a successful work of art."[10] He seems right also when he says the illustrations do not just send us back to the text for meaning but convey a complementary significance of their own.[11] The view applies well to the illustration of "The Chimney Sweeper" of Innocence. It is not the Angel with a bright key who releases the boys from their coffins, nor God, their promised father, but Christ.[12] Had Blake used the figure of an angel, he would at best have reinforced the rationalizing error of the dream, providing no new dimension of the text's meaning. At worst (if, for example, he had satirized the Angel pictorially), he might have undercut or distorted the meaning grotesquely, by mocking the child's rationalization, an unsympathetic gesture that would leave the reader small chance of experiencing very much of what the rationalization implies about how the Sweeper's mind works in the midst of great pain. Blake's point, of course, is not that the child's self-deception is an isolable "wrong" to be identified and indicted but that it exemplifies an all but unavoidable mechanism which may be undone only by those who discover its operation in themselves. His method is not to offer precepts but to engage the reader in living examples.

Though it does not mock the boy's solution to his problem, the illustration does in fact gently repudiate it, by means of a clearly identified though unexplained alternative, Christ. The distance between the two solutions is enormous, as later encounters with Blake's Jesus make clear. Recall the Jesus of "The Everlasting Gospel," for instance, who knows that "God wants not Man to Humble Himself." But the Chimney Sweeper, one realizes, is in no state to recognize the fact. Beyond the repudiation, however, the text and the illustration, considered without reference to other works by Blake, are mysteriously joined, the connection hinted, it may be, by the echo of Tom as sacrificial child whose head was "curl'd like a lambs back." Is it that Tom's white hair, in being lost, is saved, as Jesus (Matthew 16:25), no less than the Chimney Sweeper, may be said to know? The very mystery is a comment on the child's blind yearning, and yet it adds a component to the ultimate reasonableness of hope in Blake's universe.

Few of the *Songs* present characters who suffer assaults on the psyche as fundamental and direct in their effect as those experienced by the Chimney Sweeper of Innocence. But many of them in fact give us characters who endure very basic psychological affliction. The Little Boy Lost has a biological father hardly more protective than the Chimney Sweeper's. Bereft, both children cry for God the Father. The Babes of "Holy Thursday" in *Songs of Experience* are "Fed with Cold and usurous hand." In "London," infants sound the "cry of fear." The Little Black Boy is defined by the ineradicable color of his skin, and by its chief consequence from his point of view, the absence of the English boy's love. Ona, in "A Little Girl Lost," seems to take her painful sexual guilt directly from her loving father. The speaker of "To Tirzah" identifies his mother as the creature of self-deceiving cruelty who molded him.

Other songs are less obvious about the beginnings of the painful experience that helps to generate Selfhood. The Nurse of Experience, the Sick Rose, and the speaker of "A Poison Tree" are overpowered by a conditioned self that governs them. But how they become what they are is not apparent. What is clear is that the poems in which these characters figure identify a distance between their behavior and some implied ideal behavior radically different from the one displayed. Close readings in search of evidence about their painful conditioning and its spiritual consequences to them are typically rewarded in these and other poems. Even songs that might seem at first to be about social or philosophical issues primarily— say, the problem of evil—turn out to include a heavy psychological component about pain-wrought minds. "A Dream" and "On Anothers Sorrow," for example, may appear to be little theodicies. In the one, a glowworm saves the lost Emmet; and Christ joins sorrowing humanity in the other. But in fact the nominal action of the first of these songs is the substance of the speaker's dream, which controls but hardly disguises its painful content, whose "real" locus, of course, is not the geography of the dream but the speaker's mind. It is he who is afraid of being lost, and it is his dream that filters at the same time that it reveals the frightening concern and then provides the doubtful happy ending.

> Once a dream did weave a shade,
> O'er my Angel-guarded bed,

That an Emmet lost it's way,
Where on grass methought I lay.

Troubled wilderd and forlorn
Dark benighted travel-worn,
Over many a tangled spray
All heart-broke I heard her say.

O my children! do they cry
Do they hear their father sigh.
Now they look abroad to see,
Now return and weep for me.

Pitying I drop'd a tear:
But I saw a glow-worm near:
Who replied. What wailing wight
Calls the watchman of the night.

I am set to light the ground,
While the beetle goes his round:
Follow now the beetles hum,
Little wanderer hie thee home.

His dream is both the emblem of a Selfhood generated by fear and the shape that makes the reason for his fear acceptable.

The speaker of "On Anothers Sorrow" imagines a world in which all sorrow is pitied, by him, by a parent, and by God as Christ. Obviously he has experienced pain. But he attenuates the recognition of the pain of others, in consciousness at least, by placing it in the context of unusually supportive pity, a control that culminates in the identification of mortal Christ as the ultimate comforter. Formed by painful experience, his Selfhood may be said to control his way of reducing such experience. As he speaks the song, he overstates his case to the point that he implies his own doubts that pain is always modified by pity: "No no never can it be. / Never never can it be." And after an abrupt transition, which seems to intensify his doubts, he transfers the entire problem of pain ("woe," "sorrow," "grief," "fear") to the Incarnation, manipulating Christ's coming in such a way as to ascribe it entirely to God's pity for the sorrows of Innocence. The impulse is pathetically dependent. It contrives at evasion of the unpleasant thing it recognizes. Speaking out of a very different premise from mine—the redemptive value of sorrow—Bloom points out that the pattern "gets [Christian redemption] exactly . . . backwards," in that it represents an avoidance of the very suffering that traditionally marks the way to Christ.[13]

Both "A Dream" and "On Anothers Sorrow," like "The Chimney Sweeper" and "The Little Black Boy," are typical of the *Songs of Innocence* in showing us characters afflicted by pain and masking it from themselves as they struggle to survive in the fallen world. Two works written during this early period, "The Lilly" and *The Book of Thel,* provide a valuable contrast to this paradigm. (Though the second is not one of the *Songs,* of course, its date of composition and its subject make it an appropriate part of my present concern.) Both Thel and Lilly are controlled by a fiction that gives them an unusual psychological past. Unencumbered by conditioning, and yet in different ways emphatically shaped beings, they provide us with an unusual opportunity for seeing an aspect of Blake's view of the mind with reference to the formation of Selfhood, through their carefully managed perspectives.

Thel is indeed between Innocence and Experience, as W. J. T. Mitchell points out, but her Innocence is a special case.[14] When we meet her, she has had no past of the sort we can recognize. Indeed, her childhood is identified essentially in the terms of its pastoral timelessness and its biographically unencumbered culmination—her coming of age. At this point her sexuality is mortally complex, but it is achronic.[15] The Virgin of Har has escaped the kind of domestic history with which most of the children of *Songs of Innocence and of Experience* have been freighted. Obviously Blake may shape his poetical fictions as he chooses. My point is not at all that he should have given Thel a world-informed past, as he gives one to most children in the *Songs,* only that he has not done so. Her mother has not died when she was very young; she has not been made to feel sexual guilt by her father. She has not been molded by the mother of her mortal part, nor has she been deserted by her father. Similarly, the world outside the home has spared her. She has not been seized by priests, nor birched by her teachers, nor fed with the cold and usurious hand of reluctant charity, nor made to anticipate bleak existence by a pale nurse. Even dreams and ruminations upon suffering have brought no dark shadows to her life in Har, as they have to the speakers of "A Dream" and "On Anothers Sorrow."

Thel's environment has been congenial, and her sexuality, essential to the working of the poem, is conditionally assigned to her. Without it, she would not be a mortal being; with it, she is equipped to confront and apprehend generative life and the death towards which individual generative life moves. Despite its functional vitality, however, she may repudiate her sexuality by repudiating the only life in which sexuality has meaning, the life of Experience. It is not that sexuality is lightly fastened to her. Quite the contrary, during the time that we see her, it is her sexual self-consciousness—her wish to be of use to Experience—that dominates her being. But it is true nevertheless that her maker, Blake, has been careful to give her what the rest of us do not have: the power to remove herself, without dying, entirely from the object of all sexual natures—mortal life.

Her sexuality is conditional in another important way too, implicit in what I have earlier said. It seems to have a neutral or "nondevelopmental" past, to judge from the evidence available to us. Obviously her identification as someone who has crossed the threshold of sexual maturity implies antecedent sexual development. And it is true that the voice of sorrow breathing from the hollow pit speaks a complex sexual language that is in one sense or another Thel's own. Yet the poetic force of the occasion moves us to infer that Thel's recognitions at the grave plot are instantaneous. She is given to us as one deeply motivated to explore the possibilities for a life of use, a sexual life. She questions mortal representatives—Lilly, Cloud, Worm, Clay—and then she enters the world to see things for herself. But there is no indication that she brings a sexual history with her to guide, anticipate, or skew her vision of things. Indeed, the very concentration and intensity of her perception, at the grave especially, suggest the immediacy of her reading of mortal life. But her flight back to Har is the most revealing element of her story. If she had had a sexual past, the sexual present we share with her would have become the transition to her sexual future, for better or worse, or to her death. The terms of sexuality require continuity, healthy or pathological, or its utter ending. Blake pointedly exempts Thel from that obligation or that choice.

W. J. T. Mitchell has argued persuasively that the issue in *The Book of Thel* is not whether Thel has failed to enter Experience or succeeded in saving herself from the fallen world. It is rather the power of the poem to draw its readers into the problem represented by Thel's dilemma and choice, so that we share "the paradox and ambivalence which torment [her]."[16] He has so well reviewed the inconclusiveness of the evidence in support of indicting her for the failure to enter Experience, and the similar inconclusiveness of the evidence in support of her return to Har as a sensible decision, or as a decision made subsequent to her attainment to a Higher Innocence, that there is no need to review it here. In fact we shall see in a moment that Thel's psychological dynamics make it inappropriate to ask whether she should or should not have entered Experience. For now I will simply agree with Mitchell that the poem is better regarded as engendering in its readers a process of self-regard than as imparting to them a moral or a philosophical conclusion. Mitchell makes another important point about the subject matter of the poem. "What is primarily there," he says, "is the story of a young woman who questions her own usefulness and purpose in a world where everything dies or fades away, and who is given the opportunity to explore death in order to come to her own conclusions. Read metaphorically, with an awareness of its implicit contexts, *Thel* is a story of dying as growing up as being born."[17] It seems to me that Mitchell is right about this matter too—that the subject of the poem is Thel's exploration of death as intensely implicit in mortal life.

But I think it important to qualify the combination of his claims by incorporating into that combination what I have said about Thel's carefully controlled past. *The Book of Thel,* then, is a poem in which Blake gives us the chance to live with the consequences of imagining, through Thel, the world as it might be seen by a young person who is sexually mature and wants to live a useful life, and who, unlike most of the characters in *Songs of Innocence,* has not been conditioned to mitigate death's presence in the World as an unconscious psychological strategy for survival. To this claim I hasten to add that I do not say Thel has no Selfhood but that hers has been assigned to her in accordance with the special conditions Blake has set, rather than in accordance with that other Blake fiction, her development in the world of mortality from birth to late puberty. Accordingly, the perceptual mediator between Thel and the mortal world is her pristine sexuality operating immediately through the consciousness. In her mind there are no filters and distorters of self-deception like those we have seen at work in the minds of the Chimney Sweeper, the Little Black Boy, and the speakers of "A Dream" and "On Anothers Sorrow." She has been specially equipped to see something like "all" of the fallen world at once.

In a sense, of course, she is also confronting her own Selfhood all at once. Her sexuality, at work "inside" her, the ally of biological life "outside" her in the fallen world, promises death as well as life. In this context of perception, the world of her graveplot and the world of her Selfhood (and of her death) are identical. Given her unfiltered vision, which is as unprepared for defending her in a Chimney Sweeper way as it is for allowing her a glimpse of eternity beyond "the couches of the dead," she has a narrow choice between death and flight. There is no question of her confronting death and her Selfhood in the world of Experience. Blake has not provided her with the opportunity gradually to develop the self-deceiving convolutions of mind

that would, first, protect her against her overpowering perceptions of some-
thing like the "whole destructive truth" of the natural world, and, later, allow
her to confront it, bit by bit, over time, in a painful and yet endurable Self-
examination. The net effect of the poet's choices has been to make Thel a
spectator to life, as Mitchell sensitively observes about her in his comments
on the illustrations to the text,[18] but a spectator "thoroughly exposed" to the
power of death in mortal life. As we consider her unprotected response, by
contrast with the Chimney Sweeper's, we are in a position to imagine that
Blake implies not only that death seems ubiquitous at some prerationalizing
level of human apprehension but that the self-deceptions the mind prac-
tices, and the Selfhood thus produced, may be essential to the mind's sur-
vival. For a time at least, death wins either way.

Blake's interest in the mind that is too open to the world of Experience for
it to survive there does not end with *The Book of Thel*. There are evidences
of the interest, for example, in the poem "Mary," in the Pickering Manuscript,
and in Blake's letter to Thomas Butts, about the forthcoming trial for sedi-
tion, dated from Felpham, August 16, 1803, in which, however transiently,
the poet seems to include himself among the too-open minds.[19] It is chiefly
in the association of himself with Mary, by means of the line "O why was I
born with a different Face," that Blake places himself among the steadfast
and unprotected spirits of the world in his letter. Several stanzas of "Mary"
will make the point clear.

> Sweet Mary the first time she ever was there
> Came into the Ball room among the Fair
> The young Men & Maidens around her throng
> And these are the words upon every tongue
>
> An Angel is here from the heavenly Climes
> Or again does return the Golden times
> Her eyes outshine every brilliant ray
> She opens her lips tis the Month of May
>
> Mary moves in soft beauty & conscious delight
> To augment with sweet smiles all the joys of the Night
> Nor once blushes to own to the rest of the Fair
> That sweet Love & Beauty are worthy our care
>
> In the Morning the Villagers rose with delight
> And repeated with pleasure the joys of the night

And Mary arose among Friends to be free
But no Friend from henceforward thou Mary shalt see

Some said she was proud some called her a whore
And some when she passed by shut to the door
A damp cold came oer her her blushes all fled
Her lillies & roses are blighted & shed

O why was I born with a different Face
Why was I not born like this Envious Race
Why did Heaven adorn me with bountiful hand
And then set me down in an envious Land

To be weak as a Lamb & smooth as a dove
And not to raise Envy is called Christian Love
But if you raise Envy your Merits to blame
For planting such spite in the weak & the tame

But it is "The Lilly," in *Songs of Experience,* that provides the clearest instance of his concern. Like Thel, the Lilly has no human past. Unlike her, it is irretrievably mortal.

To many of Blake's readers, the Lilly has seemed to be praised for openness in love, and indeed it is. Nevertheless it is more fundamentally identified as the ideal of a being with the capacity for continuing to be its essential self in an inimical world that finally destroys it. In a limited way, it is the emblem of a being that seems to require no Self-annihilation, though it is held up to us less as a model to be imitated—it is missing a crucial dimension, in fact—than as an ideal obverse of the generality of mankind, who unconsciously surrender their true beings and their openness of vision by modifying themselves self-protectively and self-deceptively. The apparent simplicity of "The Lilly" is in part the result of its brevity.

The modest Rose puts forth a thorn:
The humble Sheep a threat'ning horn:
While the Lilly white, shall in Love delight,
Nor a thorn nor a threat stain her beauty bright.

Yet that very brevity helps to accentuate the meaning beyond the nominal one I have identified as usual, that is, the Lilly is praised for openness in love.[20] As I have said, that other meaning praises not openness in love so much as the inviolable and unconstrained expression of one's own essential nature. What is wrong with the Rose and with the Sheep is that they include a contradiction of themselves, viewed from one vantage point, at least. The Rose's beauty attracts, and, inconsistently, its thorn deters. The Sheep's humility promises peace, whereas its horn threatens. But the Lilly's nature is unviolated by any such contradiction: "Nor a thorn nor a threat stain her beauty bright."

This shift in critical emphasis from love to essentiality may seem slight, for it does not, after all, supplant the usual reading. It simply claims that the poem treats a more fundamental matter, the Lilly's consistency of presence and behavior, under which new heading the old reading about openness in love may be sustained, with modifications. Before considering ramifications of the reading I have proposed, I should perhaps offer another word or two about the reading itself. The view that sees openness in love as the governing principle of the poem seems to draw on two facts. First, all three forms of life—Rose, Sheep, Lilly—are attractive, apparently welcoming love. Then, it turns out, only one of the three, the Lilly, is what it seems to be, a welcoming lover. But all three are not potential lovers in the same sense, surely. The love represented by Lilly is very different from the love represented by Sheep or by Rose. In a way, then, it does not seem reasonable to compare them in the matter of love, as if that were the common ground. But it does seem reasonable in the matter of consistency of presence and behavior, for they do share that ground.

Viewed from the "inside" as minds, Rose and Sheep seem unremittingly defensive. Viewed from the "outside" as social beings, they seem to deny their nominal essential qualities by making themselves available only with a qualification. It is only the Lilly who is nondefensive and available as its essential self. One may say with Damon, Wicksteed, Bloom, and others that it is open to love, as Rose and Sheep are not, but it is chiefly the absence of anomalous self-defense that makes the Lilly essentially itself and therefore essentially available to others. The operative word in the last line is "stain," I think: "Nor a thorn nor a threat stain her beauty bright." The Lilly is not unstained in the sense that it does not withhold its love but in the sense that it is without psychological alloy.

On the face of it the Lilly seems to be an Innocent—not the rationalizing Chimney Sweeper kind, but one enjoying the blessed state in which people and forces outside it are continuous with itself, a state in which it sees no inimical elements in the world. If the reader of the poem concentrates on the Lilly exclusively, such a reading is inevitable. But the thrust of the poem moves one to a comparison of the three—Rose, Sheep, Lilly—a conclusion which the history of critical responses to the piece no less than the logic of its structure bears out. One might even say the Lilly is made one of a trio only so that it may be differentiated from the other two. Given the stress on comparison, and the spare, unelaborated characterizations, the Lilly is less a loving Innocent, like the Little Lamb, on whose felicity and blessedness the reader is encouraged to dwell, than it is an example of psychological consistency. Blake's interest in the Lilly extends to another important matter. It is that its unself-regarded consistency leaves it not only "unstained," but also highly vulnerable, like the Chimney Sweeper, Thel, and all of us in mortal life. In manuscript drafts of the poem, Blake includes a lion, a priest, and a soldier along with Lilly, Sheep, and Rose. The lion, like the Lilly, seems steadfast in being its essential self—"*And the lion* [shall] *increase freedom & peace*"—whereas priest and soldier are represented as behaving inconsistently with reference to their nominal definitions: "*The prist* [sic] *loves war & the soldier peace.*"[21] Sheep, Rose, priest, and soldier in a way contradict their essential identities; lion and Lilly do not.

But there is an important difference between the lion and the Lilly. It is that the lion, in the draft version, can maintain its own identity in an inimical world, not only without adverse consequences to itself, but with general benefit, it seems: "*the lion* [shall] *increase freedom & peace.*" The Lilly, however, though it maintains its identity consistently, suffers a crucifixion, as Erdman points out.[22] The flower, a day lily shown in the right hand margin of the plate, fades at day's end, having given "no thought for its life," like its prototype in Matthew 6. Blake's omission of the successfully consistent lion and his inclusion of the unfortunate Lilly increase our understanding of the nature and the value of Selfhood much as Thel's naked encounter does. If his aim had been to approve the maintenance of one's essential self, he might have preferred the lion to the Lilly in the final version, or he might have included both, without distinguishing between them. As it is, he seems to be saying that the unstained or essentially consistent being of the Lilly, though spiritually preferable to the defensive, self-repudiating, posture of Sheep and Rose (priest and soldier), is nevertheless faced with certain dangers which their self-repudiation enables them to cope with. And as for the steadfast pair, as I have said, it is the vulnerable Lilly he chooses to dwell on, not the naturally invulnerable lion, who may be understood to enjoy already those very qualities he increases, freedom and peace.

In this chapter I have paid much more attention to how the mind works as it forms a Selfhood than to the elements "outside" the mind that stimulate it to do so. Blake pretty clearly regards this formation to be inevitable and the results deeply compelling in their operations. At the heart of the matter is one's vulnerability to death in the fallen world. Normally the perception of death or its dangerous proxies cannot be borne in youth's consciousness. The Chimney Sweeper and other Innocents accordingly transform unconsciously the painful and destructive things they come up against, making them possible to bear; these children construct a Selfhood. Thel, reared beyond the limits of the fallen world, takes the opportunity to investigate it, equipped to do so with a recently matured sexuality, "nondevelopmentally" structured. What she sees makes her fly in terror, leaving us to conclude that its assault on her receptive consciousness has been so massive that she would have died had she remained. Seen from one point of view, Thel exaggerates death's presence in the world. Seen from another, she observes its presence without incorporating it into forms of Selfhood, as other characters do. The Lilly has been endowed with an inviolable (psychologically unmalleable) being, and the world destroys it. Unprotected by a Selfhood, or by the power (or the wish) to withdraw from the world, or by the lion's special strength, the Lilly is overcome. To ask about the quality of the world that so distorts the mind, or terrifies, or kills, as if that quality were utterly discrete and in no sense a function of the mind of the beholder, would be to ignore Blake's view of things. "The Suns Light when he unfolds it / Depends on the Organ that beholds it."[23] But there is for Blake a created world nevertheless, and within it numberless other worlds, physical and ideational, created by human beings.

3

Into the Dangerous World

If life has no ordering principle, it cannot be sustained, but if the ordering principle is made to fix things too rigidly, life may be contracted to the very limits of individual self.[1] To generalize the matter in the terms of the first two chapters, one might say that the formation of a Selfhood is the fulfillment of the ordering principle without which life cannot be sustained. The Chimney Sweeper of Innocence manages to control dangerous forces very efficiently, at least for the short term, whereas Lilly and Thel, each for different reasons and in different ways, do not do so. But in sustaining life, the Chimney Sweeper confines it, whereas in losing life, Lilly and Thel identify the possibility of engaging and knowing it fully.

The first two of the *Songs of Experience* represent this spiritual paradox. For taken together, "Introduction" and "Earth's Answer" imply both the need to order worldly life and the reduction of life implicit in a confined ordering. But it is not easy to understand the relationship between the order that sustains life and the order that reduces it unless we know more about the characters Bard and Earth, in whom that relationship is acted out. Though the two are only broadly representative of fallen humanity, they are at one level made available in psychological terms we can respond to immediately. Both are lonely, and both are full of the longing to overcome their isolation. Each sees the problem in different terms, and neither alone is able to solve it.

Although he is in several important ways endowed with a human psychology, the Bard is unconfined by time or place. He may be understood to embody universally valid poetic-religious truth, at the same time that he is burdened by unfulfilled desire. This complex pairing of his eternal endowment and his unfulfilled human need is reflected in his statement to Earth. As a prophet, he tries to reassure her by saying that the state of the fallen world that constrains her is also a state "given" her, apparently a useful or necessary "gift," and certainly a "gift" she can change for the better over time. As prophet, he also associates himself with the Holy Word that calls upon Earth: "the lapsed Soul / . . . That might controll / The starry pole; / And fallen fallen light renew!" In short, he seems to know Earth's spiritual state, and knows Earth has the power to "control" and "renew" it. The solution to the problem of Earth's constraining order (expressed here in the terms of light) is not the absence of order, but its control and renewal.

In his unfulfilled human dimensions, however, the Bard seems as helpless as a rejected lover: "O Earth O Earth return! / . . . Turn away no more: / Why wilt thou turn away." Whatever his prophetic knowledge may be, it is incomplete without Earth's return to him, which he seems to envisage in decidely physical terms. His regard of her is complex to say the least. She is a lapsed Soul, and all lapsed Souls. She is, as Earth, the territory in which he works prophetically to effect redemption. But she is also the Bard's longed-for companion. It seems certain that he, as Holy Word, does not ask her simply to become what he is. Clearly what he is does not make for completeness. He wants her to join and complement him, as Earth. From the Bard's perspective as prophet, what Earth needs is his knowledge incorporated into her life, so that its ordering principle may be tempered by a liberty that takes it beyond the physical limits of mere body; and from his perspective as human manqué, what he needs is her field of being, her body or control of space, which is also an ordering principle.

On the face of it, Earth is in no state to receive either the Bard's spiritual reassurances or his pleas as lover. Confused by the anguish of constraint, she sees "starry floor" and "watry shore" as physical and imaginative barriers, not as life-sustaining limits temporarily imposed on her. She is filled with "Stony dread," and "her locks [are] cover'd with grey despair." Under the circumstances, it is no wonder that she does not reply to the Bard's plea directly. Instead, she characterizes her sexual predicament, and she does so in the terms of blame. She accuses "the Father of ancient men," who through "Jealousy" constrains her.

For the most part her will to fulfillment is hostile. It accuses forces outside itself, unreflecting. But it also shows some sign of introspection compatible with the Bard's entreaty that she "Turn away no more." Her references to spring's outwardly expressed joy in the fourth stanza imply her hope for the open expression of inner life, which anticipates liberty of mind no less than of body.

> Does spring hide its joy
> When buds and blossoms grow?
> Does the sower?
> Sow by night?
> Or the plowman in darkness plow?

Fulfilled, her hope would make the Word flesh, or in less explicitly Christian terms, it would liberate her by combining the activities of body and imagination. Seen in this light, what she wants is very like what the Bard wants: the redemption of humanity in the form of "spiritual body, not as consciousness excluded from energy and desire."[2]

Earth's explicit though curtailed knowledge of her own state implies that she is closer to the beginnings of redemption than her expressions of despair suggest. Still, she represents for humanity the grounds not so much for optimism as for hope. David Erdman's reasons for identifying the reclining figure in the illustration as the Bard's, not Earth's, are good ones. But I am inclined to agree with others, for example D. G. Gillham, who believes it to be "Earth . . . , a naked woman lying with her back turned . . . from the Bard himself, hiding her beauty from him, turned from the Holy Word."[3] She is certainly turned away from us, and presumably from the Bard as well, so that she is not available to him in one sense. But apparently she has arisen from "the dewy grass," as if following the Bard's wishes, for as Erdman points out, the figure seems to be on a cloud-borne "lounging divan."[4] If she has indeed arisen, hers would not be the only illustration that complements the meaning carried by the text alone. In fact the same thing happens, as has already been suggested, in the illustrations of "The Chimney Sweeper" of Innocence and of *Thel*, and it will be shown to recur elsewhere. Here it may be understood to verify the soundness of the Bard's redemptive hope, a gentle opposition to the heavy context of her despair, which is not entirely unqualified, as I have said already.

Separate and separated though Earth and Bard may be in text and illustration, they are ideally part of one another. The complex terms of their longing imply such an ideal. So do their closely related inadequacies, and the constraints working on them. Earth is no doubt physically coerced by the "Selfish father of men," so that her blaming him may be said to have a real basis. In another sense, however, she has incorporated that coercion. One might say that her psychology *includes* the jealous guardian of her sexual life. If she were to become aware of this fact, she might be no less coerced physically, but the terms of the two songs in which she and the Bard figure indicate that she would "turn" toward the Bard as a result of her newly won knowledge. They are part of one another. Incidentally, she may already have begun to realize that her jealous guardian is, in a sense, within her. At least she listens to him with her mind's ear, as she lets us know in the tenth line—"I hear the Father of the ancient men"—an imaginative act that I take to be a good omen.[5]

The combination of the Bard's power and his deep need for Earth—it implies the insufficiency of an otherwise great being—has given trouble to some critics. Instead of seeing the Bard and Earth as two parts of a single humanity, they have explained his plea in the terms of Christian dualism. In this view, he asks Earth to give up her body for the Holy Word. The Bard's reference to "lapsed Soul," understood to imply a conventional separation of body and soul, has also been made a basis for the claim of his dualism. But the term need not be taken in its most literal Christian sense.[6] Would the Bard say the "lapsed Soul / ... might controll" its physical environment if he were an orthodox Christian? He would rather say the physical environment might be transcended. His plea to Earth, full of sexual overtones, is not for the rejection of the flesh but for its permeation by poetic intellect, with flesh recognizing intellect's presence as part of itself, and with intellect enjoying the flesh.

The Bard and Earth together provide us with a representative or universal sense for the state of the world and the means for its redemption. From the poems in which they figure, we learn it is a fallen world, marked by a division of the principles of Body and Soul, whereas in fact "Man has no Body distinct from Soul, for that calld Body is a portion of Soul discerned by the five senses."[7] What accounts for the unfortunate division is identified in part by Earth: "Starry Jealousy does keep my den / ... Cruel jealous selfish fear / ... That free Love with bondage bound." But other of her comments suggest certain psychological components of her negative state apart from the sexual, narrowly defined. She lives in "darkness dread & drear / Her light fled." She wants "emotional" as well as physical freedom: "Does spring hide its joy / When buds and blossoms grow?" She needs liberty for external action, sponsored and supported by liberty within. But it is in other songs that one finds the particulars that help to explain Earth's representative sense that she is being coerced.

As one moves forward in *Songs of Innocence and of Experience* from "Introduction" and "Earth's Answer," or backward to *Songs of Innocence,* for that matter, one sees different categories of psychological territory, which together identify the dangerous world that Bard and Earth want redeemed. At one end of the range is the household into which the child is born, with its complex protections of love and confinement. In parents one discovers loving preoccupation with offspring—in Lyca's parents, Ona's father, the speaker of "A Cradle Song," for example. But parents also confine and shape their children's minds. Having been molded by the mothers and fathers of their mortal parts, these parents pass on to their own children the crippling and yet necessary psychological heritage. Thel cannot enter Experience without it. At the other end of the range of negative influence is the natural world itself, which beyond the Piper and a few congenializing lambs, shepherds, sparrows, and rising suns, includes sobbing robbins, sorrowing wrens, lost emmets, howling wolves and tigers, and growling lions. Between these limits of household and natural world, whose psychological effects interpenetrate, are such structures as schools, churches, governments, armies, and social practices (marriage, prostitution, child labor, charity), along with their human representatives. Again, in individual minds and bodies throughout this range of territories are joy, hope, trust, faith, mercy, desire, pity, sympathy, peace, love, hate, cruelty, fear, jealousy, terror, sorrow, awe, incredulity, helplessness, despair, disease, death.

In the world of the *Songs,* parenthood is a function of a primary need to protect the lives of children, though there are a few parents who abandon them. Typically, the nature of the parents' obligation requires them to prefer physical or psychological safety for their children to self-fulfillment or truth. Lyca's parents have in some degree inhibited her entry into the world of sleep, the world of her own mind, which she wishes to explore independently as an expression of her growing maturity: "How can Lyca sleep, / If her mother weep." Though their hold on Lyca's imagination is not so great that she refrains long from going her own way, the strength and tenacity of their sense of parental obligation is identified by the utter inappropriateness of their pursuit of her, spiritually considered. Why do they enter her world of mind, where they are complete strangers? Or rather, in what sense can they be supposed to enter it? It is probably reasonable to think of their journey, for whose details there are no correlatives in their own imaginations, as an aspect of Lyca's journey. She leaves them behind to enter her own world of sleep, but she also worries about doing so: "Do father, mother weep.— / Where can Lyca sleep." And so despite herself she carries them along in dreams—"Sleeping Lyca lay; / While the beasts of prey, / . . . View'd the maid asleep"—in a form in which she remembers and understands them, that is, worried about her well-being, even in the new private territory she has just entered. In fact, her parents are her problem, the bar to imaginative maturity. Both the curious shift in Blake's interest from Lyca to her parents—from "The Little Girl Lost," in which Lyca figures, to "The Little Girl Found," in which they seem to figure—and the parents' complete absence from the illustrations to the poems, may be thus explained. Her poems are about leaving her parents behind, psychologically more than physically, which she does by carrying them along with her and neutralizing their presence in her new state. So regarded, the two poems become more intensely poems about Lyca primarily, and about the necessity and difficulty of overcoming the conditioning influence of the parents of one's mortal part, even when they are loving, nourishing, and benevolent, or perhaps especially then.

Ona's case reinforces this view. More explicitly interested in the direct expression of her new sexual maturity than Lyca, Ona too tries to leave her parents (her father) behind, but only partly succeeds. The bond between the generations is deep and fast. Its attachments are also reciprocal. The father has such a grip on Ona's emotional life that, after she has met her lover, he has only to give his daughter a loving look to induce a sense of guilt: "his loving look, / . . . All her tender limbs with terror shook." But his susceptibility to her is equally deep, as his response to her terror makes clear. If the father were to respond to Ona's guilt with anger, one would be justified in supposing the subject of the poem to be exclusively authority's coercion of young love, as Blake's opening stanza seems to say it is. But instead, he begs her to explain why she is pale and weak, and he generalizes the present emergency by referring it to the terrible history of his parenthood: "O the trembling fear! / O the dismal care!" That he trembles in fear is no more surprising than that she shakes in terror.

As the last stanza of the poem makes clear, what the old man wants most is salvation from anxiety. The "hoary hair" is obviously enough the sign of his old age. What is not clear is why his hoary hair should have blossoms, or why the blossoms should "shake"—as Ona's limbs "shook,"—because of his dismal care. The answer is that his hoary hair may give way to death before Ona has done her part to assure the continuity of family. From her father's point of view, Ona is the wavering potentiality for such continuity rather than its realization, just as literal blossoms are a promise of fruit and not the fruit itself. If all goes well, if Ona will behave prudently, as the father understands prudence and as Ona with at least one part of her being understands it, then she will support the succession of the generations. Otherwise, the father's promising blossoms, that is, Ona herself, may shake and fall.

What Ona has tried and failed to do is to take an important step towards independence, without reference to the parentally defined world in which that step may have negative consequences. From the point of view of the life of the generations, she has no right to take the step towards sexual liberty, as if it were a private matter. She ought to produce children in an environment safe for them, presumably in matrimony and the domestic setting it generates.

Needless to say, the conventional attitude that governs both Ona's response and her father's cuts deep into their psyches. "Terror," "trembling," "dismal care" indicate their intensity of feeling. What is at stake is life and death as they see things. If the shaken blossoms fall, the sequence of generational life will end. It is irrelevant that other Onas may be relied on to produce children within the domestic setting, or that Ona may produce children outside it. Despite her earlier sympathy with the open view of love expressed in the first stanza of the poem, the fundamental truth for Ona and her father is that she has threatened to violate the law of domestic security. If she were in fact to do so, the result for the father would be a fruitless life. Whatever spiritual reserves he may have, they are not apparent. He is pure "father of generation" as we see him, so that without secure progeny similarly committed to generation, his life might never have been, from his point of view. For Ona the result would be her isolation from the domestic pattern, an isolation she finds attractive for the pleasure and the freedom it affords. But she does not have Lyca's psychological depth. She has taken on more than she can handle, it seems.

The crucial point is yet to be made. If the poem is read as Blake's censure of the coercive father, a reading the last stanza, particularly, makes unlikely, the obstacle to redemption represented by "A Little Girl Lost" is reduced enormously. One has only to assign the blame for Ona's guilt to the father who reared her, encourage her to see the hold he has on her, and await the good results. Indeed, that is finally the irrational and unjust thing that must be done if one is to change the kind of distorted vision brought about by Ona's unconscious domestic molding, as the speaker of "To Tirzah" makes clear. But there is a vast difference between blaming the parent and realizing that both parent and child are victims of the same tyranny.

A close reader is made to cover the distance between the sympathies of the first stanza of the poem and the last, weighing both. In the first, the speaker sides "indignantly" with the children, who, like Ona, want the open love of Blake's "future age"; in the last, he understands the parent. The lesson of "A Little Girl Lost" is that parents and children alike are tyrannized by the domestic view of things. Both are its unconscious vehicles. The intergenerational nature of the affliction enlarges the problem represented by Ona's uncertainty about her sexual life. She is terrified when she attempts a solution on her own. And her father's complete dependence on her actions reveals his limited capacities. His fatigue with guardianship and his premonition of failure are both induced by fear. He is afraid, like the "Selfish father of men" accused by Earth; "Cruel jealous selfish fear" is at the root of his severity. As a victim, Ona's father is pitiable. As an unconscious disciplinarian who is also a responsible loving father, he will be hard for Ona to satisfy sanely. Given the complexities of confined domestic life, perception beyond the narrow view it engenders requires great imagination.

Though I shall offer a reading of "To Tirzah" in a later chapter, I wish to mention here that it is the piece above all others in the *Songs* that defines the relationship between child's and parent's domestic vision and the terrifying world that seems to require it.[8] Its late addition to the *Songs,* 1802 at the earliest, and its imagery, more nearly like the language of the prophetic works than that of the other songs, has raised questions as to the propriety of considering it along with *Songs of Innocence and of Experience.*[9] But there seems no good reason to doubt that Blake intended it as a clarification of the spirit of the *Songs* generally. The poem works by implying the psychology of the child's response to the inimical world in which he lives up to the time he repudiates his mother. Clearly, he believes himself to have been profoundly confined by her, psychologically shaped to conform to the requirements of "Mortal Life," without any concern for his need "To rise from Generation free." As he sees it, she does all this with "self-deceiving tears." The result is that she influences him profoundly in the direction of mortal and away from eternal life. Her unconscious teaching inculcates a richness and consistency of attitude in her child that mere precept could never achieve. Not only does she dominate and cruelly mold him in the self-conscious way in which one person may dominate and mold another. She also unconsciously initiates him into seeing life, unconsciously, in the way the race has come to see it over millenia of trial and error since the Fall, as a battle for survival at any cost. Her work as mother of his mortal part embeds him in a heritage of seeing with the eye rather than through it. The fallen world is in him and around him, and in a sense he has become that world.

In different ways and in different degrees so have Lyca and Ona. All three show us the tight grip mortal life has on them, through its convenient agent, their parents, who are themselves victims. All of them also have some resources for escaping the grip. The speaker of "To Tirzah" seems to know most about his relationship with his parent, in the terms of consciousness. Ona has physical daring—perhaps it is only that she soon forgets her fear—though we have no evidence for concluding that she has much understanding. But Lyca behaves in a way very promising for redemption. She manages her parents by means of the powerful metaphors of her own world of imagination, to which her parents succumb. All three young people have a long way to go, nevertheless. The household may become the place that makes the earthly family eternal, but it is typically the place that weaves its children tightly into mortal life. And yet, it is as necessary as Selfhood. In fact, it is Selfhood's most nearly complete social analogue.

The *Songs* include adults other than parents who control and shape vulnerable children. Occasionally, grown-ups are supportive, like the Nurse and Old John of Innocence, though even in the poems in which these benevolent characters figure, "the light fades away" or "The sun does descend," leaving the children on "the darkening Green." More often the controlling adults who are not parents represent the large system of things constructed by analogy with family—government, church, school, labor force. One might suppose an unconscious collusion between parents and these corrupt institutions to be at work in the *Songs*. The Sweeper of Experience observes that his parents "think they have done [him] no injury" by selling him to an entrepreneur. Then he identifies their unconscious cruelty with the deceitful cruelty of "God & his Priest & King / Who make up a heaven of our misery," by telling us his parents have "gone to praise" them. The constraining love of Ona's father is associated with "the holy book," and in "The Garden of Love" we see "Priests in black gowns" doing work like his—"binding with briars, . . . joys & desires." The Little Vagabond mocks his mother's preference for the Church over the Alehouse. It is "father & mother" who permit the School Boy to be exposed to the "cruel eye outworn" of his teacher. And Tirzah, the very epitome of the natural world and death, the ultimate coercer, simply replaces the parent in "To Tirzah," or to put it the other way round, the child recognizes the coercive parent as Tirzah. But the important fact is that the household, the world's institutions, and the natural world itself all join in the damaging and necessary work of forming Selfhood, by constraining the child's eye to worldly perception.

The Nurse of Experience is a pathetic and dangerous example of a being distorted by constraint. She has come to believe that all of life is represented by her own experience of it. Her lesson to the children—that their "spring & [their] day, are wasted in play / And [their] winter and night in disguise"—might be less effective if it were not reinforced by her "green and pale" face. One understands the psychological burden of her presence to be a heavy one, the clue being that the poem does not offer a single intimation of the children's perspective. They seem to be nothing but recipients of her barren "song." Other children who feel the psychological weight of their elders are the "Babes reducd to misery" of "Holy Thursday." They are betrayed to mortal life by adult "society" itself. It promises nourishment and fulfillment, at least implicitly—they are the wards of "holy" church and they live "In a rich and fruitful land"—but instead they are "Fed with cold and usurous hand." The signs of their reduction "to misery" are many. "Their sun," "their fields," and "their ways," which could be bright, full, and easy, are "bleak," "bare," and "fill'd with thorns," in the world of their "eternal winter."

Parents and other adults do not intentionally inflict themselves upon children. Nor do inhibited lovers intend to hurt their loves in Blake's world. Nor do foes intend to be foes and not friends. It is simply that the entanglements of mortal life produce unconscious mental operations that carry over from the most immediate victim, the person whose mind has been conditioned, to any number of secondary victims, those persons with whom the first victim shares the world. The mother of "A Cradle Song" is herself caught in a net of false hope which she unconsciously weaves around her child. The foe of "A Poison Tree" intimidates the speaker simply by being "himself." The Pretty Rose-tree cannot help turning her thorns "unjustly" against her tried and true lover. The maiden Queen (or the dreamer who dreams her) reduces her guardian angel compulsively. These errors of false being or Selfhood proliferate beyond control because they are expressions of the mind's blind will to survive without reference to any standard beyond survival. Whatever shape of Selfhood has carried us safely to adulthood, that shape of Selfhood we believe unconsciously to be the whole of us, just as we believe unconsciously that it perceives all of life. Imperious beyond understanding (with very rare exceptions), it acts out its distorted psychology in fulfillment of its need to continue itself.

The two songs that most intensely represent the powerful overflow of inner state into outer world are "London" and "The Human Abstract." Both have seemed to many readers to say that the destructive work done by humans to their kind can be undone once it is intelligently identified and its unfortunate consequences understood. And yet both poems ultimately imply such complexities of energized psychological and physical damage that one is left wondering whether it can be stopped and its root causes done away with ever.[10] Though for Blake the answer is affirmative, it is by no means simply so. "London" gives us the vision of a speaker who sees and hears by means of human symptoms—facial expressions, cries in the night—their implications for the sufferer and for the world those symptoms disclose. Though his perceptions are extraordinarily intense, they identify the context in which we all live. It is as inappropriate to say about the wanderer through the chartered streets that he perceives selectively as it is to say that Thel does. Both have been moved to respond openly, without psychological deflection of painful impressions, to the destructive forces at work around them. Thel has been prepared for her vision by means of a special past. And the speaker of "London," to judge from his intense and immediate sense of penetration and discovery, has just crossed a threshold of susceptibility to the world around him, having left his customary orientation behind. His routine guard is down, for reasons the poem does not provide. It only affirms that it is so by implying that he observes with a fresh intensity and observes what ordinarily one masks or quickly turns away from or explains factitiously.[11]

Not only are the streets of his London "charter'd"—accounted for in the terms of assigned property and power that deprive many more people than they enrich—so is the flowing Thames, whose movement away from London might otherwise have offered the imagination escape from confinement.

> I wander thro' each charter'd street,
> Near where the charter'd Thames does flow.

The consequences of this implicit demand for control of the whole world, presumably by the few in authority, is recorded in the rest of the poem as the physical and psychological reduction of the many. In fact, the repetition of "every"—"every face," "every cry," "every Infants cry," "every voice," "every ban"—implies the everywhereness of these consequences. And the other early repetition, "mark" or "marks," greatly intensifies their potency. "Weakness" and "woe" have passed into "every face" the speaker meets, the internal affliction having "marked" its human covering with its own significance. This flow of meaning from mind to face continues to the speaker, who "marks" it in the sense that he notices and gives it heed, attention, consideration.[12] The terrible movement is endless.

In Blake's London, the correspondence between inner and outer worlds is suggested in various ways. Chartered streets and river are an expression of the greed of entrepreneurs and others in authority. The weak and woeful state of Londoners comes through their faces. The speaker's sympathetic perceptions become the poem he speaks. In fact, "mind-forging" is an accommodation of inner and outer realities. In this poem of sounds, it accounts for all the notes of distress the speaker hears after he has marked weakness and woe visually. They are the audible consequences of emotional distortion, though of course the mind-forging itself has a basis in the threat of physical power over life and death, the chartered world, with its unjust distribution of good things. Cries of men, cries of infants, cries of chimney-sweeping children, sigh of youthful soldier, curse of youthful harlot, a cacophony of the distraught that culminates in the plagued "Marriage hearse," which is the cry of the speaker himself. Psychological and physical disease have everywhere come together, and in this context the promise of life has become the carriage of death.

The series in some ways implies its own continuity of disease from unfortunate harlot to man and, through marriage, to infant, youth, harlot.[13] No one is untouched and no one can be cured in the painfully lifelike fiction of this sytem. And beyond the cycle of disease in love and marriage are the intimations of another. Owners order and control the physical world everywhere—river as well as streets—supported by "Church," whose priests permit the utter exploitation of its children, and by "Palace," which calls on soldier's blood to maintain the status quo of chartered things, or, alternatively, which is to be overthrown by the soldiers it exploits after the "apocalyptic omen of mutiny and civil war . . . " appears in blood on its walls.[14] Everywhere, authority confines the lives of the many and makes use of their flesh, in terminal work or war or prostitution, as if it were the currency of the reduced world.

In the *Songs* and elsewhere, Blake understands that the world, like his London, has been brought to its terrible state by a combination of natural and social causes,[15] which promise death. For as long as fear determines psychological and physical behavior, it multiplies constraint and intensifies humanity's confinement.[16] Not only are Infants, Chimney-sweepers, Soldier, Man, Harlot controlled by death, so is London itself, futilely defined by charter against change, as if what were legally rendered "in perpetuity" could control mutability. And so are those who control the charter, taken in as they are by the greediest illusion of Selfhood, that natural life can be mastered by natural means. Obviously at one level Blake wants to save the victims of this greed. He was a reformer who certainly favored measures for improving the general well being of the socially exploited.[17] But he was not like Hobbes or Godwin, or Coleridge in the days of Pantisocracy, a thinker whose social remedies relied ultimately on natural methods.[18] Blake never dismisses the physical world. Rather he is deeply concerned that its perception by the eyes of fear, which have reduced it to a place of misery, must be understood, for the sake of the liberty from fear such understanding may bring. But the youthful Harlot's curse in the midnight streets of London is a far cry from the Bard's promised "break of day," whatever redemptive value there may be in it for "London's" speaker.

As if it were a gloss on "London," "The Human Abstract" opens by indicting a destructive social behavior, the general human willingness to provide the grounds for Pity, an ostensible virtue, by allowing people to be poor and therefore pitiable; and it concludes by locating the problem, and by implication its solution, in the "Human Brain." The opening stanza also treats Mercy as it has treated Pity, as a virtue resting on social culpability: "And Mercy no more could be, / If all were as happy as we." The transition to the next stanza is cryptic, suitable to the speaker's movement from outside world to inside mind. But it soon becomes clear that in the first line of the second stanza he is explaining how the injustices he has identified are maintained. He points out that all involved in the unconscious conspiracy to provide the grounds for pity and mercy, and all for whom pity and mercy may be felt—the poor and unhappy—are so afraid of each other that the result is a momentary social stability: "mutual fear brings peace." But this gives way in the minds of those who have the upper hand. Out of self-interest, spurred by cruelty, in whose name the unmasking speaker has them operate, the exploiters cunningly identify and pretend to believe in an otherworldly or holy basis of human affairs and they imply their own proprietary control of this holiness. With expressions of false humility, they induce the exploited, who are already frightened, humbly to accept their own adversity.

> And mutual fear brings peace;
> Till the selfish loves increase.
> Then Cruelty knits a snare,
> And spreads his baits with care.
>
> He sits down with holy fears,
> And waters the ground with tears:
> Then Humility takes its root
> Underneath his foot.

The personified Cruelty of the exploiters, having succeeded in this first part of his program of human management, extends his control through the growth of Mystery from the root of Humility. That is, he takes advantage of the fear and pliability of the exploited, institutionalizing their low status by getting them to believe their well-being is located in the context of Mystery, which seems to sponsor his authority, though it is his own brain-child. Reduced to unthinking reproductive entities which grow out of each other and no more—"catterpiller" and "butterfly"—they believe themselves nourished by Mystery. But its fruit is a lie, borne by the tree that harbors not life, but death (the Raven).

> Soon spreads the dismal shade
> Of Mystery over his head;
> And the Catterpiller and Fly,
> Feed on the Mystery.
>
> And it bears the fruit of Deceit,
> Ruddy and sweet to eat;
> And the Raven his nest has made
> In its thickest shade.

Finally, it becomes clear that the most thorough search of the natural world reveals no sign at all of this Tree of Mystery. Its only habitat is the human mind.

> The Gods of the earth and sea,
> Sought thro' Nature to find this Tree
> But their search was all in vain:
> There grows one in the Human Brain

Both "The Human Abstract" and "London" are concerned with two very closely related matters—the mind's constrained predicament and the fact that the manacles that constrain it are "mind-forg'd." In both poems, the speaker reveals his awareness that the manacles have been abstracted from the mind and methodized as institutions. In "London," the institution is chartering, the legalized acquisition of rights (property, authority) by the few against the many. In "The Human Abstract," the institution is (at the first level) religion, the church-sanctified acquisition of authority by the few over the many. But the poems complement each other. Each gives its major emphasis to one of the two matters. "London" stresses humanity's predicament, and "The Human Abstract" stresses the making and the operation of the mind-forged manacles. This division of interests, incidentally, is well supported by the illustrations to the poems.[19]

The speaker's vision in "London" identifies the "limits of opacity"; the world of night he sees there is defined by death ("Marriage hearse"), not life. Yet the very fact that his vision is as close to darkness as it is implies some liberty from Selfhood's control.[20] He sees worldly things for what they are, and he is no longer capable of turning away or accepting the intolerable as tolerable. More important, his vision is shaped so intensely that we as readers may share with him something of his clarified sense for the fullness and continuousness of destruction and pain. By contrast, the speaker of "The Human Abstract" seems to have stepped back from human anguish. From the nature of his immense practical wisdom, we may conclude that he has perceived that anguish sympathetically in the past. But as we encounter him, he is regarding it ironically. Human virtue, he says, is a luxury we make possible by the cruel handling of our fellows. As he moves quickly from human misery to his chief subject, mental operations, the immediacy and intensity of his involvement increase. Like the speaker of "London," he finds death to be the beneficiary of the mind's coercions. What death begins by nourishing—the mind's intermittent willingness to make life an exercise in survival—it ends by controlling, to the disadvantage of both outer life and the life within. Also like the speaker of "London," he understands false vision—sees how it works—and this too is a sign of his increasing power of eternal vision. But he takes a further step by denying a truly visionary correlation between mind and outer world as the basis for the holy Mystery, the archetype of institutional and familial coercion. The responsible agent is the human brain. Taken singly and together, these two poems imply both the mind's (hence the body's) enormous susceptibility to the coercive force of other minds, and the mind's capacity to discover that imposition, which is the beginning of redemptive control.

Of course physical death itself exists in Blake's world. But it is chiefly as a mind-forging threat that death appears in the *Songs,* usually in the form of one of its proxies, or as a means of characterizing the minds and lives death has come to dominate—Marriage hearse, Raven, clothes of death, coffins of black, graves in the Garden of Love, shaken blossoms, the School Boy's nipped buds and so on. The proportions of this usage correlate well with Blake's own view of things. Though he is profoundly interested in mind and world and how the two work on each other, and though he sees the heavy hand of death in both, he himself is not emotionally arrested by the fact of mortality. Even in the management of Thel, who is so arrested, Blake the artist controls her unprotected mind and presents its brief exposure to experience so as to make psychological process, rather than morbidity, the matter of interest. Aware of death's enormous power over life, including his own, no doubt, Blake can see the worst and yet understand the best the imagination is capable of in response to it. He was well able to balance his sense that Los and Enitharmon, our representatives, are "Terrified at Non Existence / For such they deemd the death of the body,"[21] with his conviction that "When the mortal disappears in improved knowledge cast away / . . . so shall the Mortal gently fade away / And so become invisible to those who still remain."[22]

Death nevertheless reveals itself in compelling physical ways for Blake. Given the "little curtain of flesh on the bed of our desire," and the "tender curb upon the youthful burning boy," can it be only mind-forging by the "Selfish father of men" that accounts for Earth's being held by a "heavy chain, / That does freeze [her] bones around"? Or is it that the natural world and the people in it are intractably mortal?[23] If Blake entertained this conclusion, he probably did so in the way most do who waver at times about vital matters knowable only in the imagination. Perhaps he had doubts. But he had a strong overriding belief, psychologically grounded, that though the world's coercers "impress on men the fear of death; . . . / Trembling & fear, terror, constriction; abject selfishness," it is possible "to teach Men to despise death & to go on / In fearless majesty annihilating Self."[24] Certainly he could teach himself well enough that about a year before he died he was able to say to Henry Crabb Robinson that he could not "consider death as anything but a removing from one room to another."[25]

But the world most people live in is a terrible place, as "Earth's Answer,"

"A Little Girl Lost," "The Human Abstract," and "London," no less than The Argument of *The Marriage of Heaven and Hell* or the song of the Bard in *Milton,* make dreadfully clear. Fortunately, certain of the *Songs of Experience* allow us to observe the psychology of self-discovery that begins one's liberation from that world. One of these is the mischievous "Infant Sorrow," from which this chapter takes its title. But others represent the mind so profoundly controlled by manacles that it seems not to have a chance to mediate between its error-filled vision of life and eternity. These apparently transfixed minds seem almost beyond salvation. It is the study of particulars identifying their state that must engage us. We know they can be saved. The interesting intermediate question is, what must they overcome on their journey?

4

Earth's Dying Daughters

Blake's opinion that "States Change: but Individual Identities never change or cease"[1] is the psychological basis of his conviction that everyone may be saved. As his poetry makes clear, the optimism inherent in this view is qualified by the difficulties in the way of salvation. Broadly identified, human vulnerability and the natural world are the elements that work on each other against the liberation into eternity. We form a Selfhood to protect ourselves from the world around us, including other humans. Then we exacerbate in the fallen world the very destructiveness that Selfhood was formed to save us from. To break this narrowing circle, some combination of grace and psychological preparation is necessary, a given moment "Satan cannot find" and the intellectual capacity to multiply its benefits "when it once is found."[2] The conscious desire to be redeemed is not enough, nor is the moment's gift of grace enough. Both are necessary.

Many of the characters in the *Songs* are to be seen struggling in this difficult and yet promising redemptive texture. Others seem to exist without much reference to it. The rationalizations that in Innocence would have deflected the pain of their lives, as well as the truth about them, seem to have broken down. They can neither rationalize evidence about their troubled lives nor come to grips with the problem it represents. They have so thoroughly incorporated their problems that they have become them.

Sometimes these spiritual derelicts are narrative conveniences, subservient to Blake's more serious interest in his principal characters. Such static characters as the Chimney Sweepers' parents, the Priests in "The Garden of Love," the Little Vagabond's mother, the Pretty Rose-tree, and teacher, father, and mother in "The School Boy" come to mind. But other characters very firmly set in their ways are themselves principles. Among the most prominent of these are the maiden Queen (more properly the speaker of "The Angel"), the Nurse of Experience, the Sun-flower, and the Sick Rose. Though a case might be made for adding other characters to these four—the Clod of Clay, Ona's father, and the mother of the speaker's mortal part in "To Tirzah," for example—they are primarily foils as Blake treats them, despite the interest he may generate in their psychologies as subjects in themselves.

The principal static or apparently static characters in *Songs of Experience* share a common psychological fate. All have depressed or mutilated sexualities, and it is primarily in the terms of sexual loss and deformation that they are represented to us. Children of Earth in more senses than one, they suffer extreme consequences of the "Eternal bane" she earlier identifies: "free Love [is] with bondage bound." Wasted or devastated sexually, their lives apparently at a dead end, maiden Queen, Sick Rose, Nurse, and Sun-flower are all weary of time or heavily constrained by what it has brought them. Whereas most of the principal characters of *Songs of Experience* are on the edge of a discovery that may bring them to a new knowledge of themselves, these four seem to be near the end of the road, and their final limitation is represented sexually.

Few would disagree that Earth, for whom there is some redemptive hope, and Thel, for whom there seems to be none, are also treated in terms of sexuality. It is worth pointing out that the measure of fulfillment for both of these characters, the good use of life, is understood to be the obverse of isolation, rather than the more sexually immediate "lineaments of Gratified Desire."[3] Not that gratified desire for Blake is unrelated to imaginative as well as to physical fulfillment. The goat's lust and woman's nakedness are both God's work. But in characterizing Earth's and Thel's negative sexual states, Blake chose terms that stress imaginative at least as much as physical deprivation. In fact, sexuality's power to move the imagination is tellingly identified both by Earth's desperation at not being able to join other minds and bodies and by Thel's terror that life will require her to do so.

Sexuality in Blake's characters is the promise that they may exceed themselves, imaginatively as well as physically. It makes possible flights beyond the protective encrustation of Selfhood. Lyca begins such a movement, which includes closely related physiological and psychological components. Her dress "loos'd," she is "naked," in body and mind as well, and alive to the possibility of a new maturity, which is represented physically by her exposed virginity and psychologically by her reconceiving her mother and father as wrested from their imaginative world and accommodated to hers. But sexuality's power to enlarge life implies its power to reduce it. For the naïve Ona, sexuality precipitates a guilt and foreboding she does not find easy to handle. Sponsored by the vision of Tirzah, sexuality is bearing children in pain and sorrow, earning bread for them by the sweat of the brow, rearing them in superstition and fear, and waiting for their circumscribed maturity to take its turn in the death-bound cycle of generation.[4] Exploited for its isolated physical pleasure, sexuality may produce "Gratified Desire," but it may finally end in "the youthful Harlots curse / [that] Blasts the new-born Infants tear." Surveying its prospects for herself, Thel is distraught by its complex alliance with death. All her senses are drawn towards and then away from life, as they converge in finding human intercourse threatening. The ear hears the signs of "its own destruction." The eye accepts "the poison of a smile." The nostril inhales "terror trembling & affright." The tongue is cloyed "with honey from every wind." And finally touch itself is sought and rejected, as if both strong desire and its negation were intensely implicit in the very anatomy of love: "tender curb ... burning boy! / ... curtain of flesh ... bed of our desire." Psychologically unequipped to mediate between the fallen world of her immediate perception and the eternal world of her ideal, Thel concludes that sexuality is fatal.

Located as it is at the heart of human longing, playing as it does on the fibers of the body and under "chains of the mind lock'd up," sexuality is the measure of life in Blake's world.[5] Its ultimate aim is psychic as well as physical unity, which includes the attributes we associate with male and female, in an integrated form.[6] But even the fleeting sense for such a completed humanity is remote from human experience in the *Songs,* except as an implicit promise.[7] Some incapacity constrains us so that we cannot yield to each other. The river of life, the "sweet River, of mild & liquid pearl," moves laboriously through corrupted channels or it hardly flows at all.[8] Apparently free, Ona makes love in a context of guilt. At liberty to choose, Thel rejects sex as deadly. Lyca's vitality carries psychological and physical elements of her sexuality forward, but the burden is immense, as the tonal weight of her songs lets us know.[9]

Of the failed sexualities in *Songs of Experience,* the speaker's of "The

Angel" is on the surface the least painful to consider, because without escaping her predicament, she has given it the finished shape of a dream. In fact, at one level, she seems to regard the experience almost playfully: "I Dreamt a Dream! What can it mean? / And that I was a maiden Queen." Other parts of her statement suggest that the dream has reduced the dynamism, and hence the pain to her, of the material it represents. In one view of herself, she is beyond sex—"he came in vain: / For the time of youth was fled"—a settled failure in the game of love, no longer participating in the struggle of human encounters. The reader may also see that part of her unconscious plan for evading her lover and putting the discomfort of courtship behind her once and for all has been to grow old precipitately. Soon after she has rejected her "mild" Angel-lover, who has courted her, presumably in her youth as maiden Queen, he returns. But she has contrived to age in dream time, so that it is too late for love:

> Soon my Angel came again;
> I was arm'd, he came in vain:
> For the time of youth was fled
> And grey hairs were on my head.

This manipulation of her aging, however, suggests not only that she has settled (tried through the dream to settle) the painful matter of sexuality by rendering herself ineligible, but that she thinks of herself sadly as old before her time. The chief evidence for this otherwise merely plausible conjecture is her lament at not having been seduced, or at not having participated in seduction: "Witless woe, was ne'er beguil'd!"[10] It is an articulate moan, outside the chain of circumstance that accounts for all the other lines of the poem and of the dream. But there is other evidence, within the "action" of the dream, which like dreams generally reveals the problem it was framed to control. Its cast of characters is important in this regard—speaker, maiden Queen, Angel mild, spinster. So are their relationships to each other.

The speaker, in the dream, conceives of herself as both maiden and Queen, and as "guarded" (her word) and courted by an Angel mild. The counters in this arrangement obviously represent both sexuality and its careful control. Maidens have not yet been lovers, but it is difficult to think of one who has been identified by the term "maiden" except in the matter of love, simply because it represents a status, one of two, in the sexual continuum virgin/virgin-no-longer. And in the context, "Queen" suggests the power to attract and dispose of lovers. The speaker's dream fantasy, which gives her sexual pleasure without sexual risk, nourishes frustration at the same time that it offers titillation and reassurances. It proposes domination of contemplated love by maiden who remains maiden (and by maiden who is Queen), rather than the fulfillment of love's impulse for union, which would dissolve the identity represented by "maiden," and here, by "Queen." That the speaker enjoys the pleasurable impulse to be a lover seems past doubt. Speaking about herself as maiden Queen, she says,

> And I wept both night and day
> And he wip'd my tears away
> And I wept both day and night
> And hid from him my hearts delight

Desire runs deep, and to the extent that the pain of its hidden existence is expressed by her weeping, desire is continuous, working on her night and day. Her tears suggest both the swell of irrepressible desire and the grief of its denial.

The Angel mild, no less than the maiden Queen, is the speaker's conception. His attributes and the expectations attaching to them are informative. He is made to serve as the maiden's object of desire, but he is not made a lover who might sense her hidden wishes and be moved by them to take a strong initiative. He is appointed to be maiden Queen's guard, but he is evaluated, illogically, for his work as lover. Finally, he is not simply a human being, but a human transformed by angelic properties—his spirit is mild, and his body is winged—with the result that he may be imagined not only as congenial and supernaturally endowed as a lover, but also quite the opposite, as inadequate or inappropriate in that role. He seems made to order for the fantasy of love, power, and rejection the maiden Queen (and the speaker) both enjoys and suffers.

In recounting his inevitable departure, the speaker does not say that he took wing, as if he had flown away in full possession of his aerial equipment. Instead, she says, "he took his wings and fled," much as if he had to pick them up and parcel them before fleeing. The intimation of dismemberment, at least of disarray, sorts well with the strength of her desire and its concealment. Even flooded with the long-flowing tears of sexual need, she keeps her secret. It also sorts well with the extremity of her armament, presumably against a second encounter: "I dried my tears & armd my fears / With ten thousand shields and spears." Besides, she also takes care to grow old "soon," disqualifying herself as a lover, just as she has disqualified him. Her fantasy ends in a triumph of suppressed desire. Angel's return is an element in the dream's denouement, much more than it is another chance for the lovers to hit it off. Both, by this time, have experienced the essentially prearranged physical disqualifications conventionally appropriate to them—impotence for him, lost youth for her. In fact, if the poem is regarded as a comment on her present state rather than as a history of events that brought her to it, it becomes a rather militant song of triumph. But her regret at sexual failure reveals itself despite her.

Few illustrations to Blake's poetry reinforce the text as immediately as does the one accompanying "The Angel." The maiden Queen, crowned, lies on her right side, her head propped on her elbow, her eyes addressing a world of her reverie, not the world around her. Her left arm is extended, somewhat behind her, with the palm of her hand, oversized, firmly rejecting the cheek, indeed the head and all, of Angel, who in the picture has been reduced sexually to young boyhood, his wings intact, but in some copies looking "like tombstones."[11] She has rigidified and in a grotesque way idealized the moment of her triumph. He is no threat whatever, and she is enjoying what seems to me a reverie, in her youthful guise. There may be pain on her face too.[12] Her triumph, for all that it fixes her in success, is a negation her systems of body and mind can maintain only at cost. The illustration seems to provide its version of a remotely potentialized contrary, for as Erdman suggests, in addition to various symbols of constraint—"vegetational entrapment," "coiled vines, viper-like, if tongueless," and the title itself, "strapped in by a tight belt down the left margin"— " . . . there is passionate coloring in the sky, his wings, and her dress."[13] Maybe Blake has left open the possibility of the speaker's salvation, in both the ambiguities of illustration and text. It is reasonable to suppose so, given his view of "the beautiful Mundane Shell, / The Habitation of the Spectres of the Dead & the Place / Of Redemption & of awaking again into Eternity."[14] But she gives no obvious clue in the text that she can get outside her error-defined self, unless the dream, an objectification of her Selfhood, somehow becomes her starting point. The conversion of maiden Queen into grey-haired spinster is a triumph of authoritative virginity which includes its own sad defeat, a hint that change is possible, though as far as we can tell, she does not recognize her sadness, even if she feels it.

The Nurse of Experience has reached final conclusions that define her inflexibly. Adams rightly says "her mental state is completely egocentric. She is locked in her own being, her own troubles."[15] Reverie may be full of the pleasure of hope or recollection. For the Nurse as she is given to us, however, it is negative, looking backwards in time to the source of her barren present and forward to its continuation. She uses this reductive pattern of thought, the instrument of a confined imagination, not only when she makes her past identical with her present and with her anticipated future. She does the same thing in making her past and the children's present identical, having assumed that their youth "now" is what she has come to understand her own to have been: "Your spring & your day, are wasted in play . . ." And she further assumes that what her adulthood

has brought her, theirs will bring them: "And your winter and night [will be wasted] in disguise." She is indeed locked into her own troubles, but she is hardly rendered inactive by them. In fact she projects and infers them energetically, though she does so in a closed system. They have become both her being and her "philosophy" it seems.

It is in a way inevitable that strong expressions of will should derive from minds like the Nurse's, which are sensitive, suggestible, and restless, as a moment's consideration of her first stanza will indicate. Like the Nurse of Innocence, she hears the voices of children on the green. Thereafter, however, she hears not laughter on the hill, but whisperings in the dale. Here are the first two lines from each song:

> When the voices of children are heard on the green
> And laughing is heard on the hill . . .

> When the voices of children, are heard on the green
> And whisprings are in the dale . . .

Both Nurses in these lines use not the active but the passive construction, as if the sounds they identify in the first line of each poem were a type of happy human signal everyone will respond to in the same way. Such need not be the case, of course, as a comparison of the second lines of the poems makes clear. But the very difference between the second lines is intensified by their issuing from identical predecessors and by the expectation fulfilled in one instance and dashed in the other. Whether the Nurse of Experience actually hears the sounds in the dale or imagines them is not as important as that they are "whisprings" and that they are "in the dale" and not "on the hill." Some depth in her has been plumbed by whisperings that link present and past.

> The days of my youth rise fresh in my mind,
> My face turns green and pale.

The experience moves her to recollect emotion, in a physiological rise and fall that requickens the life of her youth and then drops her to intensely felt defeat. The abruptness of transition from rise to fall is sounded in a broken rhythm, effected by the omission of "And" before "My face," a departure from the regular pattern of beginning alternate lines in both Nurse's songs with the word "And."[16] The shift is further strengthened by "green," which has given readers trouble; at least they have to get past a certain surprise before they can do something with it.[17] Maybe the word refers to sexual envy or (with "pale") to the Nurse's unused youth, which she regrets and resents. In any case, its visual force is in keeping with the imaginative force of the entire recapitulative process of which it is a part. The Nurse of Experience is deadened in the sense that she is confined to a particular defeated set of mind, but she is not without intensity.

Her power over the children is left unqualified by any other force in the poem. She speaks and they listen. At least whatever they may feel is not made part of the poem, though they are very much a part of the world the poem gives us. They are in her charge, they are confronted by her green and pale presence, they hear her instruction to quit play, and finally they receive her pessimistic summary judgment about their lives:

> Your spring & your day, are wasted in play
> And your winter and night in disguise.

They seem to be dominated by the force of her matted intellect. It would be hard to imagine a worse-qualified guardian of children. But given their mute lives in the poem, the incongruity of her appointment as their nurse does not register as a cruelty they endure, except abstractly, but as a reinforcement of our sense for the power of her distorted mind. It has a will of its own, but it finally controls her more than it controls them. Strong and utterly without a view of itself, it follows its bent unremittingly, reinforcing its autonomy and her isolation.

Her logic, that youth, and therefore life, is futile, may be accounted for in sexual terms. Whether in her youth she and a companion isolated themselves and whispered (secretly) in a (hidden) dale, while other children played in a group on a hill, or a couple among her present charges have disengaged themselves from the others and are so whispering, we do not know. But some such potent activity energizes her mind, and it is associated with a keenly felt sense of lasting failure. We cannot be sure that her compulsive retrospection includes precisely "humiliation, shame, and frustration," as Gillham suggests, but it clearly moves her to some such feeling.[18] Her chance for joy has been exhausted in youth, a misfortune that foreshadows her later life, and, she concludes, all later lives. More important than knowing the exact nature of the failure is recognizing the tenacity of the psychological consequences for her. The great staying power of these consequences in Blake's world implies that the experience precipitating them was secondary to the context in which it occurred, the youthful Nurse's already conditioned mind. To trace her state either backwards or forward in time is to find reasons for believing it endless, though of course it cannot be so.

The illustration includes many more or less vertical lines, in a centrally located territory that seems to be controlled by the Nurse. Beyond it, and sometimes intruding into it slightly, are burgeoning grapevines. The controlled territory itself is marked by a doorway without a door, identified by two posts with no lintel. In the doorway, seated against one of the posts, either reading or drowsing, is a girl, probably in her early teens. Despite her placement, she seems to be free of the Nurse's attentions, at least for the moment. But a boy, about the girl's age, stands upright, in well-fitting breeches and a neat short coat, his forearms and palms crossed over his abdomen. The Nurse, dressed in a simple gown represented mostly by vertical lines, roughly parallel to the posts of the doorway, is bent towards him. She has paused in the task of combing his hair, one hand poised with the comb in it, the other, also caught in the air, having just patted the firmly combed hair into place.[19] The boy seems quietly resigned to having her manage his appearance, the crossed arms as well as his face implying assimilated nonresistance. Apart from her straight gown and the arrested attentions to his hair, the Nurse is most notable for her strong-browed eye and full-bridged nose, the mouth beneath these nearly straight shapes of strength being much less fully articulated.

The picture gives the strong impression that the Nurse is actively in charge of things, but her control is limited. Whatever the doorway represents, the passage or the barrier to adulthood or to secret play or to a world without the Nurse, it is a territory she nominally controls, in ways that I have suggested. On the other hand, its posts are blurred by the vegetation of an uncontrolled world, and they support neither door nor lintel. Given these lively intrusions of plant life and the omissions of human construction, it seems hardly a barrier at all. The limits of her control are implied in another way too. The picture does not show her giving a large group of children the attention that might yield broadly effective results. Unlike the Nurse of Innocence, who guides many charges with sympathy and understanding, the Nurse of Experience has limited her constraining care to two, it seems, and her very close care to one or, at most, to one at a time. This specialization, while it diminishes her role as the nurse of many the text represents her as being, may permit her to do what she unconsciously longs to do—remake the past so that it will give her a happy present. Maybe it was for this reason that she became a nurse in the first place. It seems unlikely she will ever realize that however much she may control the boy she is grooming, she will never control the youth she could not manage, one way or another, when she was young. Has she also prepared the girl in the doorway, so that the two young people will be right for each other?

Like the maiden Queen and the Nurse, the Sick Rose is controlled by psychological forces she can neither rationalize into something acceptable,

nor come to grips with by confronting and understanding them. So deep is the control of her by these forces that the Rose cannot present her own case. Though maiden Queen and Nurse are dominated by a Selfhood, they continue to function with great strength, in a world we recognize, even through the medium of dream or reverie. But the Rose seems passive and remote. If we can credit the speaker, she needs to be told her symptoms.[20]

O Rose thou art sick.
The invisible worm,
That flies in the night
In the howling storm:

Has found out thy bed
Of crimson joy:
And his dark secret love
Does thy life destroy.

Apart from the opening line, the last two of the poem speak most clearly.
The Rose's sickness, which is destroying her life, is the result of the invisi-
ble worm's "dark secret love." Adams, Bloom, Gillham, and others have
identified the worm as phallic.[21] And such terms as "duplicity," "spectral
lust," "groping and repulsive thing," "the frustrations of male sexuality
[which] strike back," "jealousy and death" have been used to represent its
qualities.[22] Though occasionally the Rose herself has been understood to
account for the worm's presence in her bed of joy, as well as for his many
unfortunate characteristics, he is typically granted an autonomous exis-
tence as a being separate from her.[23] In these formulations, he comes as an
uninvited rapist attracted by her. Or she guiltily attracts him and enjoys
him, a distorted phallus. If the fact that the worm is invisible is taken into
account in these explanations, it is understood to be a metaphor appropri-
ate to his travelling by night and to his "dark secret love." That is, the guilty
secrecy surrounding the love of Rose and worm is taken to be a context in
which he is reasonably characterized as invisible.

These views about worm and Rose yield fine readings of the poem,
which is concerned primarily with the corruption of sexuality by guilt,
particularly the frustration and the clandestine behavior that may be gener-
ated by guilt. But I think the remoteness from her consciousness of Rose's
sexual life, suggested by the startling "O Rose thou art sick" and what
follows, all addressed to Rose in piercing terms, raises a question about
just how repressed her sexuality may be. There is a solid likelihood that
the sexual drama outlined in the poem is internal, part of Rose's dream or
fantasy life, and that she knows little or nothing about it.

The speaker's statement has been referred to as "sinewy," "bitter," full of
the "shock of terrible pity," and "begun with . . . an involuntary cry [which
includes] . . . concern, intimacy, and admiration."[24] In various ways it may

be all these things. What seems to stimulate such comments is a sense for the speaker's intensity of response to Rose. It is as if he has made a discovery about her so important for her, himself, and us that he must declare it. His rhetorically disciplined and yet precipitate statement assumes not only that she does not yet know what he has found out, but that she must be informed about it in very strong language, or at least that he finds the discovery so stark that no other language than his is appropriate to convey it. Apparently, he would rather give her the almost certain pain of his revelation than have her remain ignorant of the crucial thing he has found out about her.

The strength of his conviction might be taken to imply his belief that Rose suffers the unrealized bad effects of a real love that she is concealing from others. But it seems more likely to imply his sense that she rather suffers the bad effects of an unwillingly imagined love, about which she may know little or nothing consciously. The terrible power of his metaphors, along with his intense tone of revelation, identify the speaker as a psychologist who has recognized a new depth of mind, which his pointing out the ill consequences of a merely clandestine sexuality would not account for. But his discovery that she has concealed her sexuality from herself might well account for it.

Her sexuality is strong enough to fight through the barriers of her repression for its fulfillment, as I see it, but what she longs for is altered terribly in the passage, which is furious and full of sound: "[it] flies in the night / In the howling storm."[25] In defiance of her guilty control of it, her desire expresses itself in nightmare, having its way, which she enjoys, at the same time that she redefines its object grotesquely downward in the terms of her guilty and frightened feelings, in painful compensation for pleasure. The result is an enormously powerful tension, between dark elements whose strength increases as a function of their opposition. Desire grows, and so does the need to distort its healthy expression. Its ultimate physical locus is her bed of crimson joy, more the color of war than of love.

The illustration varies enough from copy to copy to make it difficult to identify the characteristics of the three female figures, two of whom are located on the plant where rosebuds might be, and the third, at the center of a full-blown fallen rose, the only flower in the picture. Both rosebud women seem unhappy with their state. Both conceal their faces under their hair, and neither of them seems securely placed on the stems they occupy. Not only are they implausibly located—Blake might have done something, if he had chosen, to make them little roses as well as little women—they also look vulnerable. Though both are dressed in long skirts, one has a leg thrown around her stem of the plant, and the other is kneeling and bent forward on hers. The combination of hidden faces and doubtful positions makes their holds seem precarious indeed. Above and to the left of them, yet quite close in the relative dimensions of the picture, a worm eats a leaf. (In some copies, a second worm, even closer to them, also eats.) As if to compensate for the danger of the women's blind perching, thorns cover the stems of the plant in an unnatural density, and the thorns themselves are unnaturally large. Thorns or thornlike shapes also edge the leaves, trunk, and upper portion of the rosebush's roots. But the deterrent is ineffectual. The worm close to the two women has obviously travelled a long distance over thorns to reach the leaf he is eating. And the full-blown rose with the third woman at its center, which is also heavily protected by thorns, has been reached by a worm, who in fact may account for the flower's fallen position on the ground. The woman has her arms extended, as if ready for flight from the open flower, but her lower body is inside it, and so is a portion of the worm.

One need not look long at the illustration to find connections with the text. The plant's women are both available and unavoidable, unseeing, in the path of a worm, and yet poised in a setting shaped for resistance. This ambivalence, reminiscent of the text's, which at first seems resolved in the location of the third woman, in the company of the worm, is in fact intensified by her hidden availability to the worm at the same time that she seems bent on flight. Still, the picture has a logic of its own, which both confirms and enlarges the text's meaning.

Despite the superabundance of thorns of great size, the surprise is not that the cankerworms get past them but that two women should be poised among them. Women and not flowers, they are anomalies on the stems of the bush. Are they indeed flowers waiting to be taken by the worms, or women who may stay or leave as they choose? The third woman, who is in the middle of the only bloom the plant has produced, her eyes open, and her body half committed to flower and worm and half free, provides the crucial clue. It must be that the three share a common fate. All three wait to be taken, and yet they feel the inappropriateness of their desire. No other fulfillment is available in their awful garden. All three women are at some stage of quickening the still symbol of their sexual bodies into a dynamic logic that absorbs them, so that they are, or are about to become, the Sick Rose, a human female reconceived as an expression of its own tenacious and despairing genitality. It must have been this insight that aroused the speaker's diagnostic fire in the first place.

Maiden Queen and Nurse, though caught in a psychological state that makes them its instrument, have not yet turned away from the world altogether and into themselves. Maiden Queen tells her dream, unconsciously revealing herself to us, and yet in some sense engaging us, who make up the world outside her. And Nurse, bent on controlling her charges so as to repair her own failed youth, also operates in the world outside herself. But neither the Sick Rose nor the generalized young couple associated with Sun-flower can manage to direct their energy beyond themselves, though they may move us to regard their passivity.

"Ah! Sun-Flower" is a poem about undifferentiated longing and the negative use of time.[26] Weary of time and yet obsessed with it, Sun-flower uses its days to mark time's passage, in diurnal turns of enduring futility. Unsatisfied with where it is and uninterested in whatever else it might do besides counting "the steps of the Sun," it wishes for the place where there is no time or movement: "Where the travellers journey is done." It turns out that the "where" of Sun-flower's objective, which seems to be an ideal place ("that sweet golden clime"), or a falsely ideal place, is the same "where" of Youth's pining away:

> Ah Sun-flower! weary of time,
> Who countest the steps of the Sun:
> Seeking after that sweet golden clime
> Where the travellers journey is done.
>
> Where the Youth pined away with desire,
> And the pale Virgin shrouded in snow:
> Arise from their graves and aspire,
> Where my Sun-flower wishes to go.

This identity of "wheres," strongly suggested by the speaker's parallel construction in the fourth and fifth lines, raises questions about the relationship between Sun-flower, Youth, and Virgin—where they are, what they have done with time, what they aspire to do. The last line of the poem, read as a culmination of all that precedes it, both adds to this complication of questions and helps to produce answers to them.

Stated briefly, the poem's logic of aspiration may be set down as follows. Youth and Virgin wish to go where Sun-flower wishes to go, and Sun-flower wishes to go where the traveller's journey is done, which is the very place where Youth pined away with desire and where Virgin is shrouded in snow. Because the speaker and none of the three characters is responsible for this circular identification of their journey's end, we may conclude that from his point of view, all three are filled with longing to travel to the place where no further travel is necessary or possible and where none of them need travel to get there.

Obviously the metaphors of time and place (the object of longing) are the speaker's means of identifying a state of mind in some sense shared by all three of the characters he talks about. Sun-flower makes no use of time except to count it, and to count it from a fixed position, weary of its continuation. The heavy cadences of the first two lines particularly reinforce this sense of death in life. And Youth and Virgin, sexually arrested in their primes, are in their graves, joined not in life but in death, longing not to use time but to end it. The Sun-flower as an emblem of transfixed life wasted, wishing for death as a release from the slow-paced monotony of defeat, or a worse distortion, wishing for death as the fullfillment towards which its life seems naturally to be tending, has provided the speaker with a means of seeing the barren state of the cold listless pair more acutely than he might otherwise have done. They seem caught and finished. The very penetration of his vision implies a new level of understanding, but like the speaker of "London," who also sees deeply into an aspect of the fallen world, the speaker here has not been other than saddened by his power of observation. His closing image, Youth and Virgin arising and aspiring not to higher life but to death, subverts the idea of redemption utterly. At the same time, it identifies the subversion with sexual failure. The image tells us, however, that an idea of redemption is on his mind, and that he recognizes its negation sensitively.

By contrast with the text, the illustration seems happy, even mischievous and free. Its most prominent feature, a tiny human female form, hair flying behind, arms like petals uplifted, and "root feet uprooted,"[27] straddles a spiraling tendril grown fat as it rises, and curving firmly upward at the place of contact with her. Some copies include a sun, others do not. No redemption is at hand in any case, but the transfixed aspiring to the golden clime of the sun in the text has given way to the obvious signs of liberation from earth-grave and to the energetic juncture of legs and tendril. There seems to be no clue as to how the movement from grave to happy elevation may have been accomplished. It is not a movement the speaker of the text has thought about, as far as we can tell. And neither the female figure in the picture nor Sun-flower/Youth/Virgin, whom the figure and tendril in some sense represent, seems responsible for the change. All we can say is that Blake knows the two states proffered by text and picture, and that he chose to present them to us as he has done, with a psychological gap between them, leaving us to stretch ourselves over it as we may.

Earth's daughters, not her sons, carry the greatest burden of unrelieved repression in *Songs of Experience*. As if to illustrate the quality of the sexual troubles identified by Earth in her "Answer," her daughters are represented to us as overpowered by the psychological and physical forces that define their lives. Nevertheless, this sexual differentiation cannot be read simply. To be sure, Blake's Bard of the "Introduction" to Experience, in addition to being a kind of prophetic principle, is a nominal male who knows what is wrong with Earth and explains things to her. And Earth, in addition to being physical humanity, is a nominal female so oppressed by sexual constraints that she accuses the father of ancient men instead of answering the Bard. But this paradigm of conventional male knowing and female ignorance is first enriched and then absorbed into levels of meaning having little or nothing to do with sexuality as it is usually understood. The coming together of Earth and Bard is of greater moment than the embrace of two lovers. In fact, the preconditions for the union include the fallen world's redemption. Sexuality is not denied, it is enlarged by this treatment, and it is possible to imagine that the logic of the enlargement will result in a transformation of sexuality into "non-otherness." That is, the longing of the lovers, understood psychologically as well as physically, might be taken to forecast the union of their minds along with their bodies, without reference to time.

In such a context of possibility, there is a sense in which Earth and Bard are not female and male most significantly, but parts of a whole being that longs to be complete. Viewed so, Earth may be thought of, for example, as a soul with its body-portion constrained. And Bard may be thought of as a soul with its poetry-portion curtailed by remoteness of body. But perhaps the most important point to recognize in Blake's treatment of sexually identified characters in the *Songs* is that their deep need for "another" is so nearly absolute that it implies an ideal of erotic relationship as the only means of their becoming thoroughly available to "themselves." Such an ideal destroys the conventional view that the sexual body defines the imagination within it. And it leaves open the possibility that the mental being towards which lovers aspire in wanting each other is not identifiable as male or female.

Blake's treatment of maiden Queen, Nurse, Sick Rose, and the Sunflower trio is at one level an amplification of Earth's predicament as it is identified in "Earth's Answer." It may also be seen as a comment on Blake's own sense of deprivation, expressed in the terms of women's sexual remoteness and the reasons for it.[28] But it is much more obviously and consistently a statement about the misfortune of human separateness in the fallen world, with men as well as women among those pained by it and responsible for overcoming it. Blake makes use of the sexual psychology that history has left him, but he is not bound by it, as I have already suggested. The coming together of men and women beyond the generative obligation to possess one another in a context of fear and constraint is all his concern in the *Songs*. Love without heavy chains, without thorns, without disease; love without parental intervention, without guilt, without envy, without jealousy; love without secrecy, without war, without frigidity, without genital corruption; love without religious sanctions, without the threat of death—these are the dominant calls to such a union. They also identify the dominant impediments.

These failures of sexual and imaginative completeness result from fear and the spurious mental life that derives from fear, which typically seeks control of experience, its predictability and safety. With few exceptions in Blake's world of the *Songs,* males are understood to be associated with the most effective and far-reaching forms of such futile and destructive control—the chartering entrepreneur, the mystery-making priest, the jealous father of ancient men, the representatives of the Palace, and representatives of general political and social authority. Sexually damaged and damaging youths of both sexes owe their state to this context of largely male repression. The Tirzah of the *Songs* is the great exception. To explain her categorically as a projection of corrupted male vision, part of the history of our fallen world as Blake sees it, would require the transfer of evidence from his later works to the *Songs*. Still, one might argue that Tirzah's control over her son derives from some aboriginal male miscalculation, the conversion of Death into sleep by the false vision of Mercy, recorded in "To Tirzah," suggests a priestly manipulation I shall consider. But for now I shall generally agree that in Blake's world "woman is not only the slave of the roles man and herself have forced upon her, but also the goddess man has compelled her to be, a role she has willingly accepted."[29] Her acceptance I take to be part of an unconscious strategy for assuring herself an important place in the generative scheme of things.

It would appear that if males have made the fundamental errors of intellect in the fallen world, they themselves must undo what they have done. For in the *Songs* and elsewhere, Blake makes it clear that vicarious correction of error is not possible. Sympathy and forgiveness from others support the possibility that one's error may be found out and done away with only in that they reduce the likelihood of repression in the self-probing mind. But sympathy and forgiveness are not enough by themselves. Finally the psychologically distorted (and therefore distorting) mind has to straighten itself out. In the *Songs,* males play a prominent part in this work, as the next chapter will begin to show in detail. We should not forget Earth, however, who for all the constraints on her modes of thought and language has a good idea about what is wrong with her and her children. Besides, Blake further complicates his whole division of men and women in the *Songs* by appointing men whose psychological orientation is akin to Earth's as the best of the self-examiners. No priest or entrepreneur or father of ancient men looks into himself. Instead we see men who have themselves been constrained or deluded—like Earth's dying daughters—making the inward discoveries, and this is an oblique promise that Earth's daughters will be saved. Psychologically there is no surprise in the deep kinship of temperament between the sexes. It nevertheless shows us another way in which Blake modifies the psychologies of men and women that history had given him. He clearly uses these psychologies; he gives them greater explicit value than any poet had before him; and yet they do not contain him.

5

Moments Satan Cannot Find

To prepare the way for a close look at certain *Songs of Experience* in which speakers are found in some aspect of the process of intense self-regard, it will be useful to recall a point made in the first chapter, that the minds of Blake's characters in the *Songs* vary enormously. They seem different from each other, not only in that each is encrusted by a Selfhood representing a special adaptation to the fallen world but also in that each mind implies its own sensitivity and range of understanding, qualities one divines through the Selfhood and yet recognizes as independent of it. Obviously, "mind" is no easy subject in the *Songs*. In addition to the Selfhood and the eternal identity beneath it, there are other complicating factors. The speaker's age and sex are important, and so is the context in which we encounter him— the world of "London," understood by means of the song's social metaphors, or the world of "Ah! Sun-Flower," by means of its tropisms. In addition, the reader is obliged to consider what part of the speaker's life is represented by his statement. Is it an epitome? The expression of a fading recognition? The sign of a new truth plumbed and assimilated?

If these complexities indicate critical problems, they also identify points of critical entry. They help us to decide what questions to ask about Blake's *Songs*. Though they may never lead us to collect information enough to represent all of "The Eternal Great Humanity Divine," they can be used to provide clusters of important psychological detail that allow us to survey that Humanity with considerable assurance, and to do so in terms compatible with our own sense of experience. Indeed, such questions have already led to the identification of terms that permit us a firm grasp of Blake's sense for the terrible consequences of sexual repression, the imperatives of Selfhood's formation, and the mind's willingness to rationalize wicked into good.

In turning to the speakers in *Songs of Experience* who show us the beginnings of their redemption, either by demonstrating a consciousness of their predicament, which they may be said thus to control in psychological terms, or by affording us a chance to see them in the middle of a changing vision of things, we continue to face complexities of the sort I have just identified. We will not find among them a universal presence representing all of Humanity, no Albion or Milton. And we shall have to work through the idiosyncracies of their particular state to eternal things beneath. But among these speakers there are a few who tell us about Blake's psychology of redemption significantly, because we catch them, as we might catch ourselves, having fallen out of one emotional orientation and struggling to find another. In such a threatening state of "dislocation," characters of Innocence find swift refuge in rationalization. Characters of Experience, however, seem unable or unwilling to find such a refuge. Rather they are trapped by their states, like the Nurse or the Sick Rose; or else they confront and assimilate them, discarding aspects of Selfhood and giving new vitality to their real identities as they do so. These Self-examinations are never complete in the *Songs*. But we are drawn into them, engaged by the mind and the problem it grapples with, and we may share a sense of their redemptive consequences in some degree. Whereas redemption in the major prophecies is for all places, times, and persons— wrought on a universal scale, powerful and yet sometimes remote from us as individual beings—in the *Songs* it is emotionally proximate. In *Milton,* even the sympathetic Blake character and the sympathetic Ololon cannot quite carry us to identification with Milton. But we all know the speaker of "The Little Vagabond," "The Fly," "The School Boy," and "A Poison Tree" quite well. Any one of them might be us or someone we know.

In making these few distinctions between the major prophecies and the *Songs,* I have raised a question implicitly. Do Blake's characters vary in their psycho-poetical capacity? The answer seems obvious. They vary enormously in "the gift of God" available to them.[1] Few would disagree, I believe, that Ona has less of this blessing than Lyca, and that Ona's father has much less than the speaker of "London." But it would not be easy to decide whether the speaker of "London" has more gift than the speaker of "The Human Abstract." Their visions are very different from each other, yet one mind might be capable of both. In different ways both visions require liberty from a customary view of things—enormous sensitivity of perception and enormous strength for the unwavering regard of the painful material the perception uncovers. It does not seem reasonable to ask whether the visionary capacity of either of these two approaches Milton's, say, or the Blake character's in *Milton*. All four are uniquely invested with talents appropriate to their special poetic tasks. But to ask the question and to dismiss it as inappropriate is also to recognize that all four are ultimately capable of setting Selfhood aside and looking through the eye.

Most principal characters in *Songs of Experience* are in some degree enlightened as to their psychological states (except Earth's daughters), but only a handful of them seem moved by anything like "Stupendous Visions."[2] Chief among these are the speakers of "London," "The Human Abstract," "The Sick Rose," "The Tyger," and "To Tirzah." And of these only the two last-named actually allow us to learn much about the process that resulted in their informed perspective. We can come at the details of their changing or just-changed way of seeing, either because we encounter the speakers in the very midst of their visionary experience ("The Tyger") or because their statement is an intense recapitulation of the crucial data at the heart of a recent self-discovery ("To Tirzah"). Unlike most other *Songs of Experience,* these two do not simply include elements of self-discovery, they make self-discovery their subject. At least two other songs also afford us a look at this process *as* process, "The Fly" and "A Poison Tree." Indeed almost every one of the *Songs of Experience* implies something about what happens to one's sense of identity when one is moved to see without reference to Selfhood, but a close reading of these four yields a rich model of the introspection at the heart of Blake's redemptive psychology.

At issue is the kind of psychological process that intervenes between the Clod and the Pebble, or between the earthbound Sun-Flower/pale Virgin/Youth of the poem's text and the uprooted female astride a tumescent tendril of the picture. That change between text and illustration of "Ah! Sun-Flower," left unexplained by Blake, is of a type crucial to his idea of salvation. For though no act of will can bring about the altered perspective that alone frees the children of Earth from the constraints of Selfhood, to understand the nature of the moment Satan cannot find is to be numbered among the "Industrious," who recognize and "multiply" it.[3] What is it that has moved the Chimney Sweeper of Experience to recognize his predicament, which includes his understanding the significance of his parents' alignment with God, Priest, and King? What process of recognition precedes or accompanies the speaker's diagnosis of the Sick Rose? or of the

chartered streets of London? What led the Little Vagabond to his psychologically constructive subversion, the juxtaposing regard of Church and Alehouse? One answer to these questions, of course, is that Blake the man, or Blake the poet and engraver, is capable of understanding both the states of constraint and of liberty, the "before" and the "after" of human ways of seeing and human ways of being, and so he represents both in his work. Indeed he does so. But his great concern is with the process that moves us

from the one to the other, as *Songs of Experience* no less than the pro-
phetic works make clear. Though the *Songs* do not give us visions as
complexly dimensioned as those in the long poems, they afford us a
chance to identify ourselves with their characters and to experience a
correlation between our own psychological processes and theirs.

"The Fly" is a poem about someone who is liberated from the confined
sense of his own identity (liberated from the self that dies), and who takes
the experience seriously. Yet the speaker may seem to reduce his precious
moment of freedom, first by speculating self-consciously about the experi-
ence and then by rallying from the speculation to end his statement on a
theatrical note of triumph over death. The song may be thought of as the
record of an intense vision about an apparently small matter. Given the
doubtful logic, however, of the last two stanzas, and the uncertainty of the
speaker's identity, some readers have made him out to be a self-deceiving
visionary.[4] Probably the best way to decide the issue—who or what is the
speaker?—is to try to clarify what he says and the way in which he says it.

> Little Fly
> Thy summers play,
> My thoughtless hand
> Has brush'd away.
>
> Am not I
> A fly like thee?
> Or art not thou
> A man like me?
>
> For I dance
> And drink & sing:
> Till some blind hand
> Shall brush my wing.
>
> If thought is life
> And strength & breath:
> And the want
> Of thought is death;
>
> Then am I
> A happy fly,
> If I live,
> Or if I die.

Most readers are agreed that an unself-conscious gesture that would ordinarily be regarded as of no consequence—the brushing away of a fly, probably a housefly,[5] which results in its death—has moved the person responsible for it to consider his own life and death.[6] This view may be modified by the fact that the preponderance of his feeling about himself shifts somewhat during this consideration. First, his dominant sense is that he and the fly are one. Then his dominant sense is that he, like the fly, is mortal. The two responses are by no means mutually exclusive, though setting them down as I have done suggests that they might be. The fly's death and the fly's vulnerability remind the speaker so immediately of his own vulnerability and death, his eliminated or dissolved identity, that the obvious and usual ways of distinguishing between himself and the fly are nothing beside it. The stark sense of oneness with the fly is maintained briefly by the speaker's recognition of his own previous thoughtlessness. He cannot, for a time, recover his basis for distinguishing himself from the fly. Or, seen from a Blakean perspective, he gains the ability to join the fly, having moved through the fallen boundaries of Selfhood.

It is the second stanza that contains the culmination of this obviously liberating side of his experience. Its sentences, which are questions—"Am not I / A fly . . . ? / . . . art not thou / A man . . . ?"—register not doubt, but reverent recognition of the heretofore unknown. He is of course still a man and he knows it—"thou [art] / A man like me[.]"—but he feels for the moment at least a redefinition of his usual self. The recognition of his own mortality in the fly's has moved him to feel an absence of difference between them as living creatures. At least as important, it has made him feel an absence of difference between life and death. The speaker marks his sense of identity with the fly not only as if there were no difference between a fly's being and a man's, but also as if there were no difference between a dead being and a live one: "art not thou [dead] / A man like me [alive]?" In fact, the two issues, being and mortality, are parts of the same whole. The speaker's life-defending Selfhood has fallen away, and, free of it, he has become both the fly alive and well and the fly dead, at the same time that he remains a man. He has glimpsed eternity. But the vision apparently survives at full intensity for a moment only.

The speaker's identification of himself with the fly is repeated in the third stanza. But his view there shifts in emphasis from the sensitive recognition of his unlooked-for communion with another being to an awareness of their common finitude. In place of discovery and the open regard of new experience, there is closure. "I dance / And drink & sing; / Till some blind hand / Shall brush my wing." His visionary freedom seems to have been brief, its inspiration subsiding after his one blessed look at things. The very recognition of death that freed him has here begun to shadow his consciousness. One may suppose he has no history of such experiences to refer this one to, so that it sobers him soon after it releases him.

The affirmative meaning he had given his recognition has, however, left a residue of some strength. Partly because death now troubles him, partly because he somehow understands it has set him free, he records death's visionary gift to him. At the same time, he tries to control death's power by treating it and his entire experience in mischievously comic terms. If thought is life,[7] and the want of thought is death, he argues, then he is a happy fly if he lives, in that he has experienced, as a function of newly won thought, a sense of oneness with the happy fly. And he is a happy fly if he dies, in that the same thought of identity with the unself-conscious fly makes it comically reasonable for him to claim that his death will be like the fly's.

It is, as I have said, in the second stanza that he celebrates most clearly his visionary control of Selfhood. But is there any evidence, here or else-where in the text, that he is among the industrious who can multiply the moment? It is hard to be sure. The claim that his vision accounts for a triumph over death seems ambiguous. Would he need to control death in comic terms if his vision, which is decidedly noncomic, had delivered him as he says it has? But could he enjoy himself quite as much as he does in the last two stanzas if he were not delivered in some important way? Though it is reasonable to argue, as I have done, that his movement from open recognition (stanza two) to mortal closure (stanza three) implies a visionary defeat, it is also reasonable to suppose that his second view by no means displaces the first. If the second seems to take him down to earth rather than up and out to the heavens, it may also mark the second element of the contrary that completes his vision of soul beyond the limits of body. It is not only the speaker of "The Fly" who is teased out of, and into, thought. So is the reader.

The most obvious problem for the reader who turns from the text to the illustration may be that no one in it represents the man who speaks the poem. Under the branches of a barren and forbidding tree is a mother or nurse, helping a small child to walk. He seems too old to need the kind of assistance she is giving him, and her firm grip on him reinforces the impression. Her posture, which suggests the contours of the tree trunk and curving branch, and her concentrating glance, directed at the boy, complete the impression of her control of him. As Grant implies and Erdman states, "the relations pictured are of entrapment and blind domination."[8] To the left, and not quite in the foreground, is a young girl, perhaps in her early teens. She is outside the immediate influence of the woman. But she too is almost contained, very nearly encircled, by branches of barren trees. Her back is to us, and she is hitting or about to hit a shuttlecock with a racket, but to whom (or whether to anyone) we do not know. These three—girl, woman, child—are the only humans in the picture, so that the one-sided game of shuttlecock and battledore seems pointless.

Also contained within the arching limbs of the adjacent trees, which just miss touching each other, is the double-columned text of the poem. Precisely to the right of the last two lines—"If I live, / Or if I die"—is what both Grant and Erdman say may be "a bird . . . , a butterfly, a moth, or even a bat." Its shape disqualifies it from being a housefly.[9] The creature is flying well, and the line from its tail to the vertex of its wings points right through the small opening between the not quite met branches. There is some room for escape from the forbidding enclosure, but not much. Erdman gives an interesting parenthesis to his speculation about the winged creature—"(a 'happy fly' perhaps)." To this suggested identification, which I think is correct, if one understands "fly" to mean "butterfly," I shall add that the "happy fly" is also the missing speaker.

The picture suggests to me that it may best be regarded as a series of illustrations, each representing a different order of relationship between a mortal and the world. The most prominent of these, located in the foreground, and occupying more than two-thirds of the width of the plate, is also the most bound to the fallen world. In fact, the hold of the woman on the boy too old to be helped by her—she holds him with her hand and eye—along with the enclosure made up of her overhanging body and the bare tree's curving limbs, suggests to Grant that she may be a Tirzah figure, "or the terrible crucifying woman in the first phase of action described in 'The Mental Traveller.' "[10] Controlled literally in every step he takes, under "the trees of death,"[11] the boy is being molded, or betrayed to mortal life.

Less prominent is the portion of the plate showing the girl. Occupying no more than one-fourth the width of the picture, she is not as far forward as the woman and boy, and she seems to be outside the woman's circle of control. Less close to us than they and less bound to earth, she plays a game of shuttlecock, an experiment of sorts with flights of liberty. The bird she brushes repeatedly is dead to begin with, so that her strokes may seem an imaginatively wasteful expense of energy. But the mind has no trouble in associating the action of her game and the speaker's encounter with the fly. There is as much promise of introspection as there is futility in what she is doing.

The farthest from us and from earth of the mortals in the picture is the flying creature, a very small shape against the sky, moving up towards unenclosed space. Also high up in the arboreal enclosure is the text of the song itself, as I have mentioned. One striking fact about the engraved words' relation to the rest of the illustration is the already noted location of the fly, adjacent to the final lines of the poem, in which lines mortality and immortality are made most explicitly indistinguishable in the being of the speaker himself: "If I live, / Or if I die." The two made one in the text—"I [am] / A happy fly . . ."—are again made one in the picture, but their identity is here represented by the fly, not by the man, a sign of spiritual progress. An equally striking feature of the illustration is that exactly beneath the one narrow escape route, right between the nearly enclosing branches, is the word "thought," from the line "If thought is life," a placement that stresses the poem's implicit thesis that "Mental Things are alone Real."[12] I am tempted to say that Blake would not have thought it at all sacrilegious for one to regard "The Fly," serious, mischievous, joyous, as an expression of "The Holy Word, / That walk'd among the ancient trees." He located this song about thought, life, and death "literally" among such trees, where it calls to the lapsed Souls of Earth and her children, and shows them a way. The text by itself, ambiguous in one aspect of its life-death interplay, is nevertheless fairly clear in its redemptive direction. But it becomes emphatically so in its pictorial context, where we can trace the escape from the entanglements of mortal mother and tree of death, through the movements of human-become-fly (psyche), in a clockwise ascent.[13]

The *Songs of Experience* include more richly textured visions than the one we share with the speaker of "The Fly." Of these, the only one to represent the vision as an immediate stimulus to the speaker's psychology, so that the vision becomes available to us as the process it engenders, is "The Tyger." It is very like "The Fly" in this regard, as I suggested earlier, but like "London," "The Human Abstract," "The Sick Rose," and "To Tirzah," it includes mightier elements. In "The Tyger," the speaker begins inspired by the forces that were "framed" to create the deadly Tyger, and he ends having borne and moved beyond the chief intensity of his vision of the fearful creature. In the beginning he struggles to comprehend what he has just recognized. By the end he has somehow assimilated a new truth about being and creation, such that Tyger, Creator, Lamb, and the speaker

himself are no longer the starkly discrete entities they seemed to be when the speaker first recognized the brightly burning Tyger. One might say "The Tyger" records the speaker's newfound sense that he is as deadly as the Tyger, as daring as the Creator, and as tender as the Lamb. And yet the recognition leaves the speaker in a state of heartened fatigue rather than in one of poised enlightenment. Neither he nor the reader knows exactly what promise there may be in the newly won knowledge. But it includes

his awareness that discrete inimical and discrete mysterious entiti
not be simply external to his own being.

As many have observed, the poem is framed by nearly identical st
that differ by one word only. In the place of "could" in stanza one, we ad
"dare" in stanza five.

> Tyger Tyger, burning bright,
> In the forests of the night;
> What immortal hand or eye,
> Could frame thy fearful symmetry?

The meaning of "could" in the first stanza includes doubt, uncertainty, the
need for explanation. The meaning of "dare" includes the recognition that
what at first seemed doubtful and unexplained has been accepted at some
deep level as accomplished. But many questions are raised within the
limits of these framing stanzas, which mark the movement from doubt to
some order of resolution. In addition to the explicit "Did he who made the
Lamb make thee?" these are among the questions critics have identified:
What is the nature of the Tyger's creator? What is the speaker's relationship
to him? What do the first two lines of the fifth stanza mean—"When the
stars threw down their spears / And water'd heaven with their tears"? How
and why was the Tyger created, particularly with reference to possible
apocalypse? Who is the poem's speaker, and what relationship does he
bear to the pictorial artist of its setting?

In full readings, Grant and Wicksteed offer answers to some of these
questions. Though I believe their answers need to be modified, they are
useful in focusing discussion. Grant says, "the [poem] is not a vehicle for
positive thinking, but a study in perplexity and metaphysical rebellious-
ness."[14] Having declared the "identification of the speaker in the poem to
be the most crucial problem for interpretation because unless we under-
stand his character we are unable to understand what he sees and says," he
goes on to suggest that the speaker is not Blake, but rather "an average but
also imaginative man who is almost overwhelmed by the mysterious prod-
igy he sees as a Tyger."[15]

In an extended discussion, Grant argues that the Tyger's origins are
associated with "the deep furnaces of hell," and, though ultimately redeem-
able, the Tyger of the poem itself is a creature of the fallen world of death
and generation. It is from this position that Grant offers the view that the

action of the poem is located in the center of the Christian idea of history, not at the edge of apocalyptic deliverance. Accordingly, interpretations that accept "the defeat of the stars" in the fifth stanza as the prelude to redemption are set aside as inappropriate. Though Grant goes on to accept Wicksteed's conclusion that "The Tyger" represents the view that if the Lamb is a creature of God's making, so is the Tyger, since "in making the Lamb God *had* made the Tyger—in making the Tyger, *had* made the Lamb,"[16] he disagrees with Wicksteed's conclusion that for Blake the Incarnation makes possible their reconciliation here and now.

If one assumes that the speaker of "The Tyger" is an average imaginative man, one hears the poem as the statement of a person less capable than Blake. And one may then agree that what the speaker says, Blake may, as pictorial artist, ironically repudiate. So the nominally benign Tyger of the engraving may be Blake's way of informing his reader and viewer that the speaker has been unnecessarily awed by the idea of the Tyger, a creature who however energetic in his eternal condition, has been "hammered into merely mortal form . . . , a parody of eternal vitality."[17]

And yet it is strange to think of "The Tyger's" speaker as average and imaginative. His awe is real and deep, and it is tellingly expressed. In fact, there is nothing much average about him. His questioning reveals his intense interest in an unclarified element of God's design. How can it be that the Creator of this world ordained hostility and death as the means of sustaining physical life at the same time that he ordained love? As Grant points out, this very question "continued to concern Blake throughout his life."[18] Surely, then, the speaker of the poem is a person of near-Blakean sensibility, and no lesser being.

The first four stanzas of the poem register the depth of the speaker's recognition of the Tyger's "deadly terrors," and they also register his incredulity that these terrors have been incorporated into a living form of the creation. The very quality of the recognition argues a capacity for seeing things "as they are," a fact that seems to promise the transformation of new perceptions into new understandings. But how? He begins to cope with his incredulity by trying to account for the Tyger's creation. He seeks meaning not in his starkly isolated perception of the Tyger alone—that would be frightening—but in the context of the animal's genesis, which is also his own. What hand or eye, "acting" hand or "imaginative" eye, could have made the creature? Both of the speaker's responses, the recognition that the Tyger exists and his account of its origins, are related elements of a single operation. The speaker makes no effort to repudiate the deadliness of the Tyger, nor to explain it in the handy terms of proverbial or domestic truth, like the Chimney Sweeper of Innocence or the Black Boy's Mother. He accepts the idea of the beast as terrible. On the other hand, he seems to believe that the fact of its terrible being can somehow be explained, and in terms that identify their common Creator. Inevitably, his examination of the experience with the Tyger becomes an examination of himself, during which he keeps trying to refer his disorientation to things he believes he knows, only to find that he is involved in increasingly larger and more complex sets of emotional self-definition.

In his deep recognition of the Tyger's "deadly terrors," the speaker at one level approximates the work of the Tyger's Creator, simply by seeing it "as it is." The Tyger depends on the speaker for his being, just as "The Suns Light when he unfolds it / Depends on the Organ that beholds it"[19] for *its* being. He thus accepts responsibility for the creation, not in the sense of having generated it in the first place, but in the sense of accepting the obligation to face up to its implications. In Blake's world, to see clearly is to accept responsibility for what one sees. Such seeing is the artist's creation of the world he lives in, though there exists an independent physical world as well.

This painful accommodation seems not to be entirely conscious in the speaker, but it is no less systematic and effective for that. Dislocations and changes of Selfhood result from the recognition of things in unplumbed depths of mind and their movement into consciousness. The person in whom such forces are working struggles to understand the psychological changes he experiences, but success is not always immediate. The route of the speaker's apparently subliminal control of things moves him past his perturbed recognition of the Tyger and towards the state in which he re-evaluates four representative identities in the human experience. Shocked into the deepest imaginable recognition of the deadly Tyger, he also appraises its Creator, as I have said, and, through the Creator, the Lamb. During this process of organized awe, the question "Can one imagine who made the Tyger?" yields to the question "Did the same Creator make both Lamb and Tyger?" And then both questions, neither answered explicitly, give way to the attitude one might have were the answers to both questions yes. It is not the questions as questions that are important but the state of mind that makes possible their being asked in the first place—and the continuation of the speaker's openness to the possibility that the answers are almost certainly yes.

Wicksteed seems to me right in associating the first two lines of stanza five both with "Reason and War" and with "the entrance of the Deity into earth's watery vale."[20] Though not often in agreement about the precise meaning of "the stars threw down their spears, / And water'd heaven with their tears," most critics take seriously the possibility that the lines refer both to the rigidity and constraint that Blake typically associates with stars and to a "breaking down of these barriers separating man from his own humanity."[21] Whether the deliverance is specifically Christian, as Wicksteed supposes, is less important than the fact that some kind of deliverance is identified immediately after the reference to the presumably constraining stars. In treating the lines, Grant makes two very important points. He suggests the speaker "may never be able to decide" the relationship between the first and second pairs of lines in stanza five, and he stresses that such deliverance as may be referred to by the speaker "must be an event in the future, or at best the present." Grant's conclusion about the text is that "both the Lamb and the Tyger will have their parts in [the] apocalypse, but their natures cannot be harmonized until after Armageddon during the Millenium."[22]

But as Blake's poetry teaches us to see, the harmony need not be apocalyptic; it need not be all mankind's, only the speaker's. And it does indeed take place in the present. In a strict critical sense, it is the speaker who is responsible for the fifth stanza. It is he whose mind "requires" and states the lines in their peculiar sequence. It is he who says, "the stars threw down their spears / And water'd heaven with their tears," using the past tense to refer to heaven's mercy, insofar as it is available to individual human beings in his predicament. The crucial question is not whether the redemption referred to here is universal, as Grant apparently supposes, or whether it is formally Christian, as Wicksteed believes, but under what circumstances it has become available to the speaker.

Clearly for him a fixed state of things has passed. In perceiving the Tyger as he has, he is compelled to define Tyger, Creator, Lamb, and himself anew, in such a way as to integrate them into a new scheme of things. If he is in any sense compelled to wonder whether the Creator of the Tyger is also the creator of the Lamb—"Did he who made the Lamb make thee?"—then one must conclude there was a time when he believed, however unconsciously, that the answer was no. One must also conclude he is at least on the verge of admitting to consciousness that Lamb, Tyger, and speaker are parts of a single system, however different they may be from each other. And in understanding this special unity of the Creator's devising, the speaker "accepts" the creation which is both deadly and loving, and he also recognizes that he himself includes the Tyger no less than the

Lamb. The speaker has passed from "deadly terror" to a new knowledge of the system of things of which he is a part. This implies, equally, his passage to a new knowledge of himself.

In the final stanza, "dare" for "could" is the first gloss on this new condition; the apparently benign Tyger of the illustration is the second. "Could" in the context implies the speaker's willingness to search for the capacity to create the Tyger. "Dare" implies the knowledge that a creator is available, the remaining question having to do with the "willingness" to create it and what such willingness represents. The movement from "could" to "dare" represents no shift in objective fact, only a changed perception of the speaker. Having wondered "could?" he has come to imagine "dare!" with all it implies for the power and morality of the Creator and himself. He has acknowledged the fact that the Tyger's fearful symmetry has been framed. And in some sense he himself has framed it within the limits of his statement, whose final stanza returns to the central issue, with "dare" representing something like the *fait accompli,* in which he has participated. The mystery of the Tyger's creation has not been dispelled, but it has been looked at, it has provoked a recognition, and it has been incorporated by the speaker into a new sense of himself. At least some of his Selfhood has died to make way for new life, and he may now be able to deal with the deadly state of things he has dared to see.

The illustration in which the poem is set extends its verbal implications by various means. Several of the picture's elements are important in this regard. First, the Tyger is not fierce, but neither is he a cat essentially; rather, he is a cat with human features. Second, his stripes and those of the tree, the tree of Death,[23] are almost indistinguishable, in some copies, especially where the two merge. And finally, it is the tree, somehow joined with or possibly sprung from the Tyger, that dominates the picture, though it seems to do so with less than maximum potential force.[24] Obviously the Tyger first recognized by the speaker of the poem is very different from the Tyger depicted in the illustration. It seems reasonable to try to explain the difference between the two by assuming a development in meaning from the first to the second. Having written the poem, Blake provided for it a pictorial setting appropriate to its "ultimate" meaning. If the salient elements of the illustration are indeed a Tyger with crucially human features, a merger of human Tyger with the tree of Death and of the knowledge of good and evil, and the dominance of the world of the poem by that tree in a somewhat attenuated form of itself, then important correlations between text and picture are apparent.

First, the poem's tentative softening of the starkness of discrete and sometimes opposed entities is brought to partial resolution in the picture. In "The Lamb," speaker, child, Lamb, and Savior are identical: "I a child & thou a lamb, / We are called by his name." In "The Tyger," speaker, Tyger, Creator, and Lamb are in the first instance supposed to be very different. But the perceptual progress of the speaker, as it is indicated by his questions about the Tyger's Creator and the Lamb's, implies the inaccuracy of this initial view. The speaker of "The Tyger," who begins by seeing the Tyger as a unique terror, recognizes in the course of his thinking that he, with the rest of creation, is himself the Tyger in some sense. He who made the Lamb made the Tyger, and He made man as well, who is both Lamb and Tyger and more. In this perception of created things, it is appropriate that the human Tyger should not look terrifying; it is likewise appropriate that the tree of Death and of knowledge should be associated with the Tyger and with the speaker, who is responsible both for the creation of the Tyger and for the knowledge represented by the tree.

The discrete forces earlier perceived have not been so assimilated that the speaker has returned to Eden. (Lamb and Tyger do not lie down together.) Quite the contrary, what he has achieved is a new consciousness of his state, which includes his knowing that the world is overhung by the branches of the threatening tree associated with the loss of Innocence and death. The illustration represents the fact that in the face of this recognition, the distance between himself and the Tyger who engendered the terrible vision in the first place is greatly closed. Both seem less than significant beneath that tree, though they give it life (the tree seems to grow out of them), and though the speaker has shown he has the visionary capacity to move beyond its inhibiting implications. Paradoxically increased and diminished by his experience, the speaker is for the moment in the condition of rest and hope. The deadly tree's leaflessness, the eagle of genius above, and the pink sky beyond are among the signs of his potential redemption. But his changing definition of himself is the chief sign, though it must for the moment appear to arrest hope entirely.

6

Good and Evil Are No More

Unlike the speakers of "The Fly" and "The Tyger," the speakers of "A Poison Tree" and "To Tirzah" have assimilated their experiences well enough to recapitulate them in an orderly way. The recapitulation is hardly dispassionate in either poem, but it is clear from the conclusions each speaker has reached, including what may be called his sense for the completeness of the experience he recounts, that he is in conscious control of its content. Like the speaker of "London," the speakers of "The Fly" and "The Tyger" are revealed to us in the midst of their visions. We do not know what they will do "afterward." Like the speaker of "The Human Abstract," the speaker of "A Poison Tree" and of "To Tirzah" tells us about his vision well after the moment of its chief intensity.

These last-mentioned speakers have all looked steadily into a typically concealed or only fleetingly regarded matter—the systematic management of humans by humans who are priests, foes or friends, and mothers. What they uncover not only subverts conventional notions; much more disturbing, it also leaves the speakers in possession of an active point of view most of us do not keep alive, even if we share it in some degree. Unlike the speakers of these poems, we find it acceptable to allow our knowledge of human control to subside, except in times of emergency, when we run the risk of being imposed upon. Having seen to our protection, we rest. But these three seem to find their conclusions valuable beyond such practical concern. They behave as if they had taken seriously the lesson of the devils

on behalf of the just man in *The Marriage of Heaven and Hell.* Their
tenacity has led to a certain discomfort with them among critics.[1] It may be
that the speakers are simply full of answers recently provided by experi-
ence, so that we may suppose their intensity of recollection will diminish
appropriately over time. That would be natural. But it seems more reason-
able to suppose that they have made a discovery extensive and deep
enough to change their psychology radically. I suggest that each of them
has in a different way disturbed a fundamental element of conventional
morality, after which he is unable to return to customary notions of good
and evil as the basis of his behavior. Each is morally alone. But having been
thrown clear of the conventional way of appraising human relationships,
each is also morally independent.

The speaker of "The Human Abstract" has discovered in the "human
brain" both the fear that makes the control of humans by their fellows
possible and the cunning will to exploit the frailty. The speaker of "A
Poison Tree" finds in himself the will and the capacity to destroy an enemy.
The speaker of "To Tirzah" realizes that his greatest spiritual enemy is his
mother. In such a context of human susceptibility and destructiveness,
which is not an aberration but a commonplace thing, good and evil be-
come useless moral categories. But their inevitable abrogation by the
mind that has become painfully enlightened ought not to be taken to
represent a preference for conventional evil over conventional good.
Rather, it is in the nature of discovering the imposture of conventional
good that the discovery seems to be a triumph of conventional evil. Blake
himself may have contributed to this sense. It is not always easy to remem-
ber that the devils of *The Marriage of Heaven and Hell* are meant chiefly to
confront the angels. Whenever the status quo is overturned by devils, who
are actually the agents of Energy, it seems for a time that evil triumphs, but
in fact it is only that the categories of conventional morality have been
nullified by an imaginative act. Considered psychologically, the speakers of
"The Human Abstract," "A Poison Tree," and "To Tirzah" have discovered
in their own experience a reason to deny the distinction between good
and evil, which neither benefits the life of the imagination nor accounts for
how the mind works beyond its constraining limits. But in making this
discovery, they enlarge rather than reduce their spiritual dimensions.

"A Poison Tree" may appear at first reading to be a poem about the
destructive consequences of repressed feeling.[2] Not telling one's wrath
may seem like nursing unacted desires. Indeed, much of the poem seems
to support this reading. Fears and deceitful wiles in the mind of the

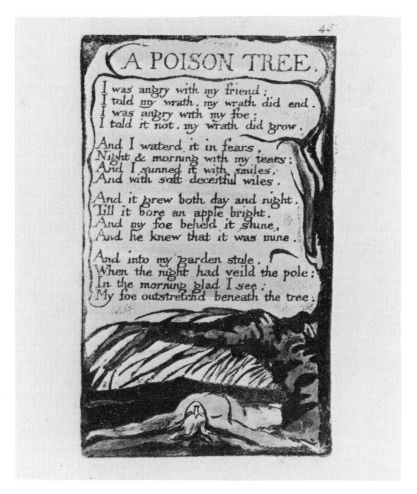

speaker maintain the life of inhibited wrath, which thereafter bears a deadly apple. The evil garden seems to have a vitality of poison beyond the speaker's control. But whereas one would expect the speaker to suffer as a result of its terrible flourishing, it is the foe who eats the apple and dies. And it is with uncomplicated joy that the speaker witnesses his dead foe: "In the morning glad I see; / My foe outstretchd beneath the tree." It does not seem reasonable that in Blake's world repressed feeling should culminate in the pleasure of glad relief.

A closer look at a matter I have already mentioned may help the attempt to sort out these details. The speaker, from the beginning of the poem, has a remarkable grasp of the incidents that make up the psychic event he talks

about. Indeed the symmetry of his presentation suggests the obvious bene-
fit of hindsight: "I was angry with my friend; / I told my wrath, my wrath did
end. / I was angry with my foe: / I told it not, my wrath did grow." He speaks
not of what is, but of what has been, and in the process of doing so, he
selects events from the past to secure the clarity that results from compar-
ing friend and foe as objects of anger. Even more clearly indicative of past
experience is the completeness of the process represented by the growth
and fruition of the tree of wrath and the consequent death of the foe.

The speaker's command of the details of his experience suggests his
gradual resolution of a psychic difficulty in proportion as understanding
and control increase. Though he is beyond fear in the poem, the speaker,
when he left his wrath unspoken, was afraid; on the other hand, the
speaker who sees his foe outstretched beneath the tree is happy, rather
like a jubilant devil in *The Marriage of Heaven and Hell.* In the first
condition, he receives the energy of assault; in the second, he directs it
towards his foe. The speaker's tone itself may be regarded as a function of
the experience completed and recapitulated, a triumph recalled, rather
than the "language" of the events as they originally emerged. Though the
means by which the change in attitude and capacity is achieved are not
absolutely clear, enough of the process is apparent to make a reasonable
conjecture possible.

First, the watering of suppressed wrath and the sunning of it with smiles
and deceitful wiles imply a consciousness of the problem. The speaker
seems both to have concealed his anger and to have nourished it, and
though he is at this early point without the means of coping with his foe,
the very fact that he can later recapitulate the process argues his increasing
self-knowledge. That which grows as a result of momentary repression and
nourishment is an interior garden world, imagined by the speaker to be
attractive to the foe as sinner: "And into my garden stole, / When the night
had veild the pole."

The speaker has become the creator and proprietor of a perverted Eden,
into which the foe will be seduced and a poison apple offered to him. This
growing sense of power to control events "may be part of his recognition
of himself as deceitful and wily," as Gillham seems to suggest.[3] In a way, the
clear and growing shape of energy that has been neither expressed exter-
nally nor repressed makes of the speaker a minor Satan, comic in his
manipulative control of things but by no means trivial. What he might have
rationalized in Innocence eventually flourishes in Experience, and it gives

him a devilish strength. One result is his ability to murder; another is his stomach for accepting the murder with pleasure.

Despite what I have suggested about the internalized foe and the garden's interior flourishing, there is a special sense in which the speaker's growing power is paralleled by its increasing application to exterior events. One might say that it is in the nature of a recently acquired awareness that it look outward. But the reader of "A Poison Tree" has much more than that to go on. The entire tone of the poem suggests the speaker's pleasure in recounting an experience that might have ended badly but turned out well. As he informs the world that it used to include among its inhabitants a foe who frightened the speaker back into himself, whereas now the foe is dead, the speaker displays a confidence that he can shape external events. It is "in the morning," the start of a new day, that he concludes the action of his interior adventure, which has brought him to the threshold of outward things. At this point there exists for him a continuity of inside and outside the mind, the chief indication that he has come to understand and make use of the threat of repression. Without this understanding, his unexpressed anger would have cut him off from the world outside. With it, the inhibiting foe of the real world is redefined, and so are the real world and the speaker's relation to it.

Then too there is the growth of the apple itself to chart the course of the speaker's process of response to the foe from frightened inhibition to murderous expression. The apple grows, the tree that bears it having been cared for by the speaker. The fruit is the culmination of the speaker's partially self-guided interior process. It is the ultimate, gradually appearing symbol of the diabolized Garden in which the speaker, an emerging Satanic principle of sorts, having been imposed upon, comes to turn his will upon the imposer.

As I have already suggested, the speaker bears an important relationship to the devils of *The Marriage of Heaven and Hell*. In *The Marriage*, written during the same period that saw the production of *Songs of Experience*, Blake urges all just men to do what is done by the speaker of "A Poison Tree." It is precisely the just man's history that he has been imposed upon and that shortly thereafter he was shown how to overturn the imposition by calling upon energetic forces within himself that derive from a new way of seeing things. Incidentally, his "history" includes the perception that "A dead body revenges not injuries." Of course both the speaker of "A Poison Tree" and the just man, even in their diabolized forms, are less potential murderers than they are persons grown aware, like Thel, that a state of war characterizes such human intercourse. The liberty to imagine all things, including the murder of one's enemy, is the devil's primary right in *The Marriage*. But then his opinions also include the view that "the most sublime act is to set another before you."

Several elements in Blake's illustration of "A Poison Tree" extend and reinforce the reading I have offered. Chief among them is a portion of the tree Erdman identifies as "a hand [just above the fourth stanza] that seems to grasp the trunk above it as by the leg of an elongated human torso."[4] A hand there seems unlikely. I suggest the element may be seen more readily as the head of a rather happy-looking serpent, from whose mouth is issuing a giant forked tongue, part of which underlines and brackets the poem's title and part of which extends the entire length of the poem to become continuous with the *y* of "My" in the last line. It is as if the Serpent of the Garden of Eden has been represented in a benign and useful aspect, sponsored by the special occasion of the speaker's apple-bearing triumph over repression and self-deception. The speaker has not so much murdered as he has discovered himself capable of murder in his heart.

His garden, *his* tree of the knowledge of good and evil, *his* serpent, *his* deceitful behavior, *his* dead foe, *his* promise of a new day, *his* completed poetic statement. All these are functions of the speaker's pictorially unending and extensively possessive "My." But he is neither proprietary nor murderous, finally, though the world of his new imagining includes the possibility for both. Indeed, the speaker of "A Poison Tree" has himself endured a death, the death of that part of him that fears the foe too much to express anger towards him. He is in a state that allows him to know he can move beyond the Lilly's passivity in the face of emotional danger. In a limited sense, perhaps, he has overseen the marriage of heaven and hell within himself. He has confronted and assimilated at least a part of the hostile world of Thel's grave plot, redirecting the death it threatens from himself to the foe. Still, his redemption is only partial.

"To Tirzah" is the song above all others that displays knowledge of the relationship between Selfhood's way of seeing things and the deadly world that seems to require such perception. Though in fact it may not be as direct in its penetration of this relationship as "The Human Abstract," "To Tirzah" provides a more extended treatment of the matter, and it does so in psychological terms that are more accessible to most readers, even though the terms have their own difficulties. Its late addition to the *Songs*, probably 1805 (1802 at the earliest), and its imagery, more akin to the language of the prophetic works than to that of the other songs, have raised questions in the minds of some as to the propriety of considering it along with other *Songs of Experience*.[5] But as I said earlier, there seems no reason to doubt that its addition, however late, was intended in the spirit of clarification.[6]

> Whate'er is Born of Mortal Birth,
> Must be consumed with the Earth
> To rise from Generation free;
> Then what have I to do with thee?
>
> The Sexes sprung from Shame & Pride
> Blow'd in the morn: in the evening died
> But Mercy changd Death into Sleep;
> The Sexes rose to work & weep.
>
> Thou Mother of my Mortal part.
> With cruelty didst mould my Heart,
> And with false self-deceiving tears,
> Didst bind my Nostrils Eyes & Ears.
>
> Didst close my Tongue in senseless clay
> And me to Mortal Life betray:
> The Death of Jesus set me free,
> Then what have I to do with thee?

I wish to preface my reading of the poem with two generalizations, each of which I shall consider briefly. They may be regarded as both premises for the reading and propositions to be tested by it. First, Blake's Christ crucified is an important symbol for salvation, and Blake's Christ is a human teacher whose deeds and sayings identify the means of redemption. He was not crucified so that we might be saved by Him as a direct function of faith. Second, the natural or "corporeal" world is for Blake a fiction, but it is also a reality to be dealt with and brought to proper perspective by a vision beyond the control of Selfhood.

One may read *Songs of Innocence and of Experience* carefully and yet come away with the conviction that even when they treat religious motifs, they do so with a secular emphasis. Part of the reason, of course, is that Blake satirizes church and priest in many of the songs—"The Garden of Love," "The Chimney Sweeper" of Experience, "London," "The Little Vagabond," "A Little Boy Lost," and "The Human Abstract," for instance. Another reason, however, is that Blake's genuinely religious sense is unusual in its operation. Routinely religious people apply their religions to events. Blake derives his religion from events, with the result that he, and not some abstract idea of the sacred, seems to be its sponsor.

Blake's Christ, for example, forgives "sins" in order that "sinners" may explore all possibilities for themselves, without the psychologically coercive fear of God's retribution. "The Everlasting Gospel" implies this mission clearly: "God wants not Man to Humble himself"; the verses also call on us to "Awake [and] arise to Spiritual Strife," so that we may "see with not thro' the Eye." In the last Memorable Fancy of *The Marriage of Heaven and Hell* we are told that his Christ also breaks at least six of the Ten Commandments Himself, exemplifying His conviction that moral prescriptions do not teach wisdom and that they may actively inhibit learning. Blake's view of the crucifixion too is unusual. He seems to have thought Christ the man had no business meddling in politics, and he deplored the physical crucifixion: "But when Jesus was Crucified / Then was perfected his glittring pride."[7] But for Blake, Christ's dying into life is nevertheless emblematic of what every person must do psychologically to move through Experience, past the rationalizations represented by the speaker of "The Chimney Sweeper" of Innocence and "The Little Black Boy," past the pain and terror of Ona and her father, past the first incapacity of the speaker of "The Tyger" and of "A Poison Tree." That movement requires one to risk the perception of things "as they are," without a compromising self-defense. What Thel beholds for an instant and then flies from, we must look at steadily until the beholding destroys the very Selfhood our minds developed to protect us from such beholding. It is an all but impossible task; and yet "To Tirzah" may make it seem easy, if one understands the poem to mean that one need only call upon Jesus to be saved. The "death of Jesus" in the poem stands for the possibility of redemption in the movement through Experience, not for vicarious salvation.[8] "Every person his own Christ" is the requirement of Blake's redemption, though at one level this issue is complicated by the relationship between individual and universal man. Rather than recall the conventional hope attaching to the death of Jesus, the reader of "To Tirzah" does better to consider the speaker's liberating discovery about his mother's deadly hold over him side by side with Ona's terrifying guilt in confronting her father. The speaker dares to see and indict the very thing that makes Ona shake.

Closely related to Blake's view of Christ as an emblem of visionary possibility is his view of the natural world as a variable obstacle to the vision of eternity. We have already seen that some of the characters in the *Songs* see through the eye and not with it, for example, the speakers of "The Fly" and "The Tyger"; and in different but nonetheless penetrating ways, for example, the speakers of "A Sick Rose," "The Human Abstract," "London," and "A Poison Tree." It should seem obvious that vision through the eye is at the heart of the speaker's concern in "To Tirzah." But in fact his terms concerning the natural world are so explicit—"Whate'er is Born of Mortal Birth, / Must be consumed with the Earth / To rise from Generation free"—and the poem itself was added to the *Songs* so late that at least one critic has argued that Blake is calling for a literal and direct repudiation of the physical world in "To Tirzah."[9]

The illustration supports such a reading. A dying young man seems to be half assimilated into the earth, his legs being no longer visible. On the robe of an old man, bent over the dying young one and offering him the contents of a pitcher, are inscribed the words (from 1 Corinthians 15:44), "It is Raised a Spiritual Body." The starkness of address to the matter of death as the corollary of spiritual freedom, in text and illustration, may be taken as a stimulus to the conclusion that Blake calls for a literal repudiation of the flesh and of the world, and a conventional Christian faith in Jesus. Such a point of view might refer us to the death of Jesus that sets one free, the necessary physical death of all who wish to rise free of generation, and the death of the spiritually raised young man in the picture. But the address to death also suggests an alternative. Blake here seems to have intensified his frequent correlation of the vision of death and vision through the eye, which I take to be the chief subject of "To Tirzah."

It is the difficult second stanza that provides us with the psychological setting in which the speaker's experience is located and with evidence for understanding what has happened to him. That setting has already been made familiar to us in "Earth's Answer," and in the "Introduction" that precedes it, where it is similarly set forth in sexual-spiritual terms of constraint. In "To Tirzah," however, constraint is given a genesis and a history. Both more cryptic and more full than Earth's explanation of humanity's state, the explanation in "To Tirzah" can be interpreted explicitly. The stanza says that the sexuality of men and women has its current basis in shame and pride; it is not eternal sexuality, as presumably it might be, but temporal, having been defined by the fall of Adam and Eve. It follows from this temporality that men and women came to maturity, grew old, and died in the post-lapsarian world, or were threatened with that fate ("Blow'd in the morn: in evening died"), until "Mercy changd Death into Sleep." The fate of Adam and Eve—death in the world and all our woe—being too hard to bear, they and their progeny would have been unable to get on with their painful lives, except that Mercy changed death into sleep. Obviously the act of mercy may signify the deliverance from death in the form of heaven "beyond" mortal life, and in a way it does. But in the context of the poem, which has to do (1) with the need to face death and (2) with the unfortunate state of one whose heart, nostrils, eyes, ears, and tongue have been shut or silenced, the implication is strong that the incapacitated one is being kept by his mother's conditioning from doing his proper work— facing death in some immediate sense. Given this logic, we may conclude that Mercy has anticipated Tirzah's work, the betrayal of vision to mortal life. The obvious inference is that Mercy's change of death to sleep was an antispiritual act generating humanity's capacity to deceive itself about the state of things in the fallen world. Tirzah has done her crippling work self-deceivingly ("with . . . self-deceiving tears"), the speaker has until a very short time before been self-deceived, and in fact the whole race has been enabled to face life, however sadly, as a result of the power of self-deception. It is only *after* Mercy changes death into sleep that the Sexes "rose to work." Without this psychologically confining act of mercy, they might not have been able to get on with life at all. As it is, they get on with it in a very limited form of itself. It is ironic that the very gift Adam and Eve secured by means of their transgression—a knowledge of good and evil from eating the fruit of its tree—is the gift they and their progeny must forego in order to survive. But of course they could not have known the knowledge would include the fact of death.

The speaker of "To Tirzah" has been placed in Earth's history and bred to join the Sexes working and weeping in a world of death they cannot recognize for what it is. The speaker's mother of his mortal part has constrained his sight, hearing, smell, and speech, denying him both a clear perception of things and the possibility of full human relationships. She has also molded his heart "with cruelty," a sustained coercion to judge from "mould," reminiscent of that other Cruelty, who "knits a snare, / And spreads his baits with care." Her reductive work on his senses has apparently been systematic, for all that it is done with self-deceiving tears. It is as if she derives it from some terrible pattern of which she is the blind, remorseless continuator. Though only the title explicitly associates the mother of the poem with formal religion, she is obviously an embodiment of the principle of the control of other minds.[10] The operation of that principle through her has constrained her son to settle for mortal life, to the exclusion of imaginative things, as Satanic or as priestly an outcome as one can think of. She has not explicitly taught him that Death is Sleep, but she has confined his imagination beneath a Selfhood of numb senses, so that it leaves the false conversion of death into sleep unregarded.

The speaker's unexplained awakening includes both a quickening of his senses and the recognition that they have been systematically weakened. And yet somehow freed from his conditioning, he has grasped the wisdom packed into the first two stanzas. As I have said, they include discoveries of the imagination that identify the plight of Earth and her children, and, of course, the very state the speaker has left behind. His insights are brilliant and economically stated. What precipitates them we do not know. But the burden of his transition is still upon him, we may conclude, or he would not repudiate his mother for her part in perpetuating the constraints of the fallen world as strenuously as he does. From it we learn the force of his recognition of the power she has wielded over him by means of her unconscious duplicity. It is his mother who has betrayed him to mortal life. She, who gave him natural life, took it, and molded it to natural ways, paradoxically preventing him from seeing that death is at its center. Unconsciously ("naturally") committed to making *his* mortal life bearable and safe so that mortal life itself may survive, his mother has prevented him from seeing what Thel recognized.

"The Death of Jesus set me free" has a meaning for the speaker that somehow represents the speaker's movement from confinement to liberty of vision. It is, after all, death that the speaker must face to do the spiritual work at hand, and it is apparently through Jesus that he does it. To the reasons I have already given for supposing he finds an exemplar rather than a refuge in Jesus, I shall only add that the speaker's question, "what have I to do with thee?" is a variation of Christ's words to His mother in John 2:4. In delivering very nearly the same words to his mother, the speaker imitates Christ, but he does not pray to Him; for both, the question marks a dramatic choice for eternal over mortal or generational life.[11] Similarly, the speaker may be understood to imitate Christ in the matter of death; he faces death, but he does not anticipate deliverance as a result of Christ's sacrifice on his behalf.

Blake's replacement of the final plate in early copies of *Songs of Innocence and of Experience* with "To Tirzah" and its illustration also implies his wish to emphasize the secular or human or psychological aspect of what is clearly a religious experience—rising, through death, from generation free. Originally the concluding plate (with no text) showed "a spiritual body borne aloft by winged cherubs."[12] In the arrangement of the *Songs* that concludes with "To Tirzah,"[13] one sees a decidedly human figure, attended by human figures, two women and an old man, dying into the earth, and no sign of the "majestic androgynous figure [in the traditional attitude of prayer] upborne by six winged cherubs," as Keynes and Raine regard the original last plate.[14] As I have already mentioned, the legend on the old man's robe says, "It is Raised a Spiritual Body." But the fact of rising is represented by human dying. It is the spiritual labor and its pain that are stressed, not the glorious aftermath. And instead of winged cherubs, the sponsoring symbol of this human dying into life is "a vine-like branch that bears seven red or yellow or pale green apples,"[15] the color and the number and placement varying from copy to copy. It is in the garden of the knowledge of good and evil, with perception's constraints removed, that the speaker is set free by the death of Jesus, having like Blake's Jesus of "The Everlasting Gospel" realized that the Inculcation of Moral Virtue is spiritual death, and having like Jesus repudiated its chief inculcator, the Mother of his Mortal part.[16] Free of her conditioning, he is like Jesus (and Thel) in mortal jeopardy, but he is also in a state in which he can learn to adore his own humanity,[17] though the *Songs* for the most part hint at this possibility only by deploring its opposite.

This remarkable character, whose redemption is made uniquely promising in the *Songs,* not only by reason of his complex psychological identification with Jesus but by reason of his "complete" knowledge of Earth's history, gives us no certain clue about the reason for his conversion. If the death of Jesus has set him free, why did it not set him free at some earlier (or later) time? In the absence of an answer, I turn again to the apparent contradiction that Blake calls on us to save ourselves, and yet he says we can do nothing "of ourselves."[18] If there were no explicit evidence, it would be reasonable to speculate from his work generally that he had no interest in the problem of free will philosophically considered, for the simple reason that analytical conclusions, however sound, cannot be incorporated into the ongoing life of the spirit. But Blake separates himself from the conventional idea that will is the choice to obey an all-powerful lawgiving God. In so doing, he breaks with the tradition of Paul, Luther, Calvin, and Boehme.[19] He rather regards such "choice" as unconscious yielding, grounded in superstition and fear, yielding to tyrants like Tirzah, Cruelty of "The Human Abstract," and Urizen, who represent both a fixed point of view and the coercive need to bind others to that point of view. Will is not liberty of choice in Blake's world. Directed or willful actions are, quite the contrary, unconscious and tyrannical, with the tyrant no less than his victim carrying out the commands of some imperious defensive psychology, necessary for a time in every life but ultimately wasteful.

In what sense then is it possible to mark well the Bard's words in *Milton,* which are the essence of our redemption? Obviously not by directing our actions of mind and body along some preconceived route. That would be to behave in accordance with the directions of Selfhood, when in fact the blessed moments that Satan cannot find are precisely moments during which Selfhood's power is suspended. How then may we be numbered among the industrious, who multiply such moments, so that they renovate other moments, as Blake tells us we may be? All we know is that the answer is not to be found in a program of action adopted and executed by the will. That would be to call upon the Selfhood to undertake the very work it was created to subvert.

It might seem reasonable to ask whether Blake may not be calling on a self "beneath" the Selfhood. But if one follows that lead, the problem of will in Blake becomes the problem of self. Though I shall have to look at that problem later, in attempting to explain the relationship between individual and universal redemption in the prophecies, to do so here would not be useful.[20] What is wanted at any rate is a sense for the quality of change experienced by Blake's characters when they are freed from the constraints of Selfhood. We need a sense for the *process* of such change rather than what a philosophical inquiry inevitably produces, a means of judging its value with reference to some fixed principle. If Blake's poetry makes such a process familiar to us, we may feel easier with its operation in our own experience. Have we not all killed the fly and wondered about our death in his? Have we not all met some tiger in the forest of the night and paused? Blake's poetry asks for no act of will. It offers recognitions and their aftermaths, so that our own interior worlds may seem less strange to us. To "mark well [his] words" is not to be directed to an act of will, but to be led to a recognition of what is somehow already available within ourselves, though unregarded.

The nature of the being, abstractly considered, that may be said to quicken these unregarded potentialities within is less immediately important than the nature of its perceptions. We understand very little about the speakers of "The Fly" and "The Tyger" that can be made available to others who might want to know about Blake's redemption. We cannot, for example, abstract the speakers' experiences and then offer the result as a method of reducing Selfhood's hold on the imagination. But we can imagine the dissolution of their usual psychological orientation as they somehow become continuous with the fly and the tyger, and wonder about the connection between their dissolved Selfhood and their simultaneous perceptions of an unpremeditated universe. All the Memorable Fancies of *The Marriage* encourage us to such new perceptions. At one level in this "movement" is a sense of disorder, fright, and awe. At another is a recognition that life is vast, complex, mysterious, not at all well explained by the formulations of Selfhood, which are implied by the disorienting experience to have been reductive. It is in their nature to be reductive. The "sequence" of these two levels of response may be represented as a liberation from the fallen world, which in the first poem is brought to symbolic resolution, the human speaker being transformed into fly and then into a psyche escaping from the nearly enclosed corrupt garden. But the culmination of this movement is inevitably qualified in that the body of the transformed human abides in time until death, and in time it needs some sort of ordering principle that contains its energy. (In a way the body is itself such a principle.) Quite different from the speaker of "The Fly," the speaker of "The Tyger," a humanized tiger of sorts by the end of the poem-picture, seems to identify his immediate post-visionary life by the signs of pause in spiritual activity. We need not choose, however, between the soaring butterfly of the first work and the enlightened and yet fatigued creature of the second. Indeed we must not do so. Both represent an important aspect of the movement away from Selfhood. There is a sense in which every dissolution of Selfhood identifies and achieves a new liberty. But every dissolution also identifies new spiritual work, which cannot be undertaken except from a reorganized psychology. "The Fly," with its illustration, represents a completed experience of Selfhood's dissolution. "The Tyger," with its illustration, represents the continuity of such experience.

It would be incorrect to conclude from what I have said that Selfhood is the intractable representation of the body's need to protect itself against mortality, so that imaginative progress away from Selfhood is followed by Selfhood's reassertion of control, unless the flight from Selfhood is absolute. It is rather that life, which is endless in its range—it always requires mental war—needs an order, just as it needs freedom from constraint. Though in many ways not comparable, the two songs "The Fly" and "The Tyger" represent these contraries. The transformation from man to fly to butterfly seems absolute; it suggests the ultimate liberty from constraint. But the transformation is located in a world that warrants comparison with that of the speaker of "The Tyger," who pauses, unable to epitomize his experience. Though he has not yet "bound" his new outward circumference of energy, it seems fair to conclude that he will do so.

In referring to Selfhood as Satan, as he does in *Milton,* and in associating the terms "Negation," "False Body," and "Incrustation" with each other and making them all the equivalent of "Selfhood,"[21] Blake has contributed to the sense that Selfhood is somehow an isolable entity. He may seem to treat it as an entity again when he says that it "must be put off & annihilated alway."[22] This hypostasizing usage notwithstanding, it is wrong to think either of Blake's Selfhood, or of the eternal Identity "beneath" it, as if it were a fixed thing. Each represents a category of dynamic psychology, and each penetrates the other. At its most stultifying, Selfhood binds nostrils, eyes, and ears, and encloses tongue so that the senses work within the limits of their conditioning. In moments Satan cannot find, Selfhood is "visited" and "displaced" by eternal Identity. But Selfhood cannot be extirpated once and for all.[23] It is dissolved only for a time, and then it must pull together a new shape of things, which serves as mediator between us as subject and the world as object. The new shape of things may well include more of eternity, so that to think of the new shape as Selfhood's doing may be inappropriate. But the very nature of the aspect of mind that works to give meaning to experience makes it inevitable that dynamic forces will be rendered stable. Our beings struggle continually to transform that which has *been* into that which is *known.*

This view of Selfhood, as an aspect of mind that may be saved through transformation by degrees rather than done away with once and for all, sorts well with what we have seen of rationalization and repression in the *Songs.* As I have suggested, the two imply a hierarchy of Selfhood's domination of the psyche, with repression allowing for no conscious intercourse between subject and object, and rationalization allowing for at least distorted conscious intercourse. The Sick Rose gives no conscious meaning to sexuality (she represses it); the Nurse of Experience gives negative conscious meaning to sexuality (she distorts it); Lyca seems to begin but not to complete the displacement of her sexual inhibitions. The view of the Selfhood as gradually and continually redeemed also sorts well with Blake's insistence that even the Elect must be saved. Their rigidities, like Reason's, represent a state "Created to be Annihilated & a new Ratio Created."[24] It is a succession of visions and revisions that accounts for the movement away from the fallen world and its Tirzah-wrought perception.

The way to eternity seems clearly marked, available to mortals as an act of imagination. But however complete the imaginative act, it must be renewed, time on time. Milton, Luvah, and Albion labor through many deaths before an ultimate redemption is effected.[25] Blake's own spiritual life followed the same pattern.[26] It is in the sequence of dislocations of Selfhood, or of some other "ratio" of meaning, that intimations of eternity are available to us mortals:

> The Infinite alone resides in Definite & Determinate Identity
> Establishment of Truth depends on destruction of Falsehood con-
> tinually.[27]

Obviously there is a crucial difference between one who has experienced the dissolution of Selfhood and lived on to see "a new Ratio Created" and one who has not. It seems fair to suppose that neither the speaker of "The Fly" nor of "The Tyger" can be the same as he was before his vision. Each has glimpsed eternity and the possibility remains alive in his past as a token of inspiration, not of memory. More important, the new shape of Selfhood, less defensive than the old, is a living promise that the undefined object of human longing is in some important sense a reality beyond the fallen world, and that we may one day attain it "forever." Of course it is also important to realize that the speakers are different men who have been through different experiences. I have already implied that the speaker of "The Tyger" may have had more to face up to than the speaker of "The Fly." As must be apparent, however, I have not wished to diminish the speaker's experience in "The Fly," and I do not wish to do so now. He clearly has got past perception *with* the eye, in seeing himself and the fly as one, in life and in death. But his vision draws fewer vital elements together than the other's does. And yet whatever the differences, both must feel a new liberty from old unconsciously adopted ways of thinking about themselves and the world, as well as what may be regarded as a new sense of responsibility for vision through the eye. When what one has understood to be the ground of one's being gives way, one is very likely to question all ground. In this activity, the recognition of further risk to one's emotional bearings may well produce fear. But the recollection of the wider world into which one was propelled when the old world was lost brings hope. Dying to be reborn, psychologically conceived, is an activity that engages and taxes all the mind's resources.

Though the speakers of "The Fly" and "The Tyger" do not seem to have as much conscious knowledge of the mental operations that account for their visionary experiences as do the speakers of "A Poison Tree" and "To Tirzah," their songs raise questions that place them among the sizeable company of characters in *Songs of Experience* who distance themselves from received opinion psychologically. Out of their deeply felt experiences, the speakers of "The Fly" and "The Tyger" come to speculate about the moral nature of the universe. Are all mortals equally holy? is a question implied by "The Fly." Did God intend that life should feed on life in a world that includes, perhaps requires, love? is implied by "The Tyger." It is a commonplace of Blake criticism that the *Songs*, especially *Songs of Experience*, question conventional values. The speakers of "London," "The Human Abstract," "The Little Vagabond," "The Garden of Love," and "The School Boy," for example, all point out systematic failures in human behavior, raising hard questions about the status quo. Instead of concurring in the indictments the questions imply, however, one may more reasonably consider the psychological significance of the fact that the questioner is able to raise the questions. Both the visionary's sense of fear and his sense of liberty and hope may be clarified in the terms of this psychological content, including the metaphors of death that are part of it.

At the most obvious level, one's repudiation of church, school, parents, government, social role, and sexual code implies one's psychological tie to the thing one repudiates. In giving up that tie, one agrees to exist between identities. In the extreme of this process of redefinition, one may be thought of as without a worldly or generational identity, like Thel or the Lilly. Given the nature of Self-annihilation as a long-term process that cannot be the result of a single visionary confrontation, there would seem to be little danger that someone between identities would feel anything like Thel's unqualified sense of death's immediacy, much less suffer the "real" death of the Lilly at day's end. But such risk is at the heart of Self-annihilation. Psychologically potent categories like mother, religion, government, work, love, and so on define us to ourselves in powerful ways. The definition of course confines us, but it also makes us secure. Even to have questioned seriously some element of its underpinning is to have considered the idea of changing oneself.

In raising questions about their parents' alignment with the social practice of chimney sweeping, with the Church, and with school, the Chimney Sweeper of Experience, the Little Vagabond, and the School Boy take a step in the direction of psychological independence, a step away from their conditioned identities or Selfhoods. We are not told just how far they go in their repudiation—they do not go as far as does the speaker of "To

Tirzah"—but we know that they must have reconceived their inevitably internalized parents, who are understood by them to be on the side of the status quo and in some sense against the children. The consequent loss of support to the children's definition of themselves, though by no means slight, is nevertheless limited. All three remain embedded in the very social context they have begun to question. One might say they are children who must remain where they are only because their social choices are fixed by others, but in fact, their view of themselves in Blake's world of the *Songs* might have been as radically independent as the view of "A Little Boy Lost"—"Nought loves another as itself"—and they might have suffered a cruel fate like his. Instead, the Chimney Sweeper at least pretends to be happy enough to dance and sing; the Little Vagabond wants only to convert the Church to another social institution, less constraining than the Church, the Ale-house; and the School Boy continues to reason with his mother and father, as if he still believed he could make them his allies: "O! father & mother, if buds are nip'd, / . . . How shall the summer arise in joy?"[28]

But more than a few characters in *Songs of Experience,* having begun to question the world around them, continue to do so until they stand outside it, no longer defined by its ideas and attitudes. The speaker of "To Tirzah" is, of course, one of these. We understand that he is giving up Selfhood as a function of his discovery that self-deception, duplicity, superstition, blind love of natural family, fear, the desire to control other people, confined perceptions—all the dark convolutions of Selfhood—are owing to our fallen-human incapacity to look at death.

The rich and complicated psychological context in which Selfhood is thus made and unmade has been well represented and its secular implications preferred to its orthodox Christian ones. But apart from certain references in my reading of "To Tirzah," I have not yet considered whether the explicit connection between death and rebirth—dying into life or Self-annihilation—is simply Blake's version of the often-cited Christian paradox, as it is offered in the First Letter of Peter, for example,[29] or whether Blake provides us with evidence for explaining the paradox in psychological terms. As many of my comments have indicated, the characters in *Songs of Experience* who most seriously question the world around them, and by implication themselves, are closely associated with the language of death, which is somehow made a part of their new recognitions. The speaker of "London" sees the city without blinders, and he concludes by finding its cycle of life sponsored by the death of "Marriage hearse." Free of conventional preconception, the speaker of "The Human Abstract" sees to the center of the human brain's creative duplicity, which he represents as a tree in which the Raven of death nests. The speaker of "The Tyger" pene- trates the conventional view of good and evil, Lamb and Tyger, and his vision, pictorially represented, concludes with his "becoming" the Tyger, in some sense, merged with the "Tree of Death."[30] The speaker of "The Fly" enjoys a vision that delivers him from his conventional view of himself, and the interim between his definition of himself as a finite mortal and his new definition of himself as an immortal butterfly is marked by the fly's death and his own. The speaker of "A Poison Tree," who frees himself from an inhibiting fear, encounters death in the form of his willingness to murder an internalized enemy.

If the fallen world is the world of death, and these characters are repudi- ating that world as a false ground of their being, why should death, which they are presumably leaving behind, somehow mark their redemptive progress? The Christian view that in order to live we must die may seem to provide a good answer. The death of Jesus, endured in expiation of sin, the root cause of death, is universally applicable from the traditional point of view. He died that we all might live beyond death, and accordingly it is in death that we find spiritual life. Even doubt as to such a deliverance need not nullify its power to save us.

> For we know that Christ being raised from the dead will never die again; death no longer had dominion over him. The death he died he died to sin, once for all, but the life he lives, he lives to God. So you also must consider yourself dead to sin and alive to God in Jesus Christ.[31]

Though these verses are a strong statement of faith, they are also a reassur- ance to those who may hesitate to accept them, afraid to face the death of the natural being in themselves. Given this context of belief and reassur- ance, it would be unsurprising if a Christian were to face death full of faith in the redemption, full of fear at the prospect of the natural being's dissolu- tion, and full of the sense that to accept death is to reaffirm the kinship with Jesus.

One might well claim that Blake's persistent conjunction of redemption and the metaphors of death in the *Songs* and elsewhere derives from this Christian heritage. Yet the derivation would fail to take two closely related factors into account, both of which may be reconciled to Christian interpre- tation only with difficulty. The first factor is Blake's strong implication that

redemption is available in the midst of physical life.[32] The second is his
practice of explaining or implying religious truths in psychological terms
that are both consistent and thorough—sufficient for salvation without
reference to the tenets of orthodoxy. In fact, Blake's psychology of redemp-
tion accounts both for the relationship between death and Selfhood's for-
mation, and between death and Selfhood's annihilation. It does so in such
a way as to make his use of various metaphors of death emotionally appro-
priate in redemptive moments, with death not only recognized starkly as a
coercive influence that shapes our fallen life but also experienced as the
visionary's own dissolution of Selfhood. Thel, who has had no gradually
accumulated experience, and therefore no Selfhood, sees the fallen world
without a protective filter, and what she sees in this unprotected state is
death.

At the first level, physical survival, the Selfhood may be thought of as a
mental faculty that protects us from this, the world's most threatening
force, without our knowing that it does so. Tirzah has seen to this protec-
tion in her son, whom we encounter at the moment of his discovery that its
unconscious invention by fallen man and its unconscious inculcation in the
minds of the young, generation by generation, are owing to fallen humani-
ty's incapacity to look death in the face. At the second level, the achieve-
ment of eternity, we confuse Selfhood with life. *In Blake's world, doing
away with Selfhood inevitably exposes us to death, not only because we
give up our defenses so that death comes at us but also because, however
irrationally, we believe the dying Selfhood is our "true self" dying, and we
are terrified.* It is for this reason that Self-annihilation is an endless work
among the living. Our resistance to such dying may be explained in Chris-
tian terms, but it is, without such explanation, of a piece with Blake's whole
psychology. Whenever our protective mechanisms of Selfhood are threat-
ened, we feel threatened, and we resist. To the extent that our resistance
succeeds, the sense of death's threat to us subsides. Recall, for example, the
Chimney Sweeper of Innocence. But if for some reason we do not resist,
like the speaker of "The Fly," we experience the loss of Selfhood as expo-
sure to death, in a degree appropriate to the order of the threat. And to the
extent that our diminished Selfhood results in our increased perception of
things "as they are," we are closer to eternity, and we feel that our move-
ment towards it has been effected by a passage through death, as indeed it
has been in the life of the mind.

As I early observed, there are, broadly speaking, two metaphors of death
in the *Songs.* In "London" and "The Human Abstract," for example, death is

at the center of the worlds the clear-sighted speakers identify—the world of the city and the world of the mind. Though other characters at the height of their clearest perceptions also recognize death in the new worlds they see—the speakers of "The Fly," "The Tyger," and "To Tirzah"—they are, in addition, *themselves* identified with dying. To distinguish between the two metaphors as if they were quite discrete is reasonable enough. After all, to see death is not the same as to die. But not to understand that they represent psychologically continuous or related recognitions in Blake would be to miss an important point. Thel's perception makes it clear that to recognize death in the world outside and to feel oneself threatened by death constitute a single psychological reality, so that the metaphoric identification of either by a character may be said to represent some order of that character's recognition of both. Close readings of the *Songs*, as I have tried to show, can reveal the enormous range of the forms of those recognitions in human consciousness, from utter lucidity to grotesque distortion. But that great variety, which exhibits Blake's grasp of many sorts of mind and many sorts of experience, ought not to mask the fact that Selfhood's mute premises are simple indeed, intellectually considered. They all have to do with the triumph of biological life over biological death, at whatever cost in vision through the eye. Anyone who either sees it clearly, as at the center of the natural world, or imagines it keenly, as one's own dissolution, is at a crucial visionary turn in Blake's universe. Yet the vision is almost impossible to maintain long enough for its truth to be applied to our daily lives and become a part of it.

7

From *Songs* to Major Prophecies: Some Continuities and Differences

For anyone who reads *Songs of Innocence and of Experience* as I do, the prophetic books, especially the later prophecies, are a source of both critical reassurance and critical uncertainty. They increase one's knowledge of Blake's anatomy of human behavior, but relative to the *Songs,* they may reduce the opportunities for understanding it in the terms of explicit daily experience. We must go to *The Four Zoas, Milton,* and *Jerusalem* for knowledge of the fourfold mind as Blake sees it—its parts and their origins, their autonomous and their relational activities, their terrible movements towards eternal death and eternal life. But Blake does not lead us into this universe of the mind as he leads us into the *Songs,* where the antechamber is a poetical version of the world we live in or think we live in. Instead, in the prophecies, he thrusts us into the middle of the mind as it is, the whole universe, without the reassuring signs of familiar things. In denying us this sort of help, he lessens the chances that we will reduce what we behold into preconceptions, the "meanings" we carry with us wherever we go. At the same time, he increases the chances that we may invent an ultimately abstract system for understanding what he says there. *Songs of Innocence and of Experience* refer new discoveries to old psychic orientations represented in recognizable forms, so that the result is a spiritually invigorating commerce between new and old. It is hard for a close reader of a song to avoid the profitable contribution of private experience to the occasion of the reading. But with few exceptions, the action of the great prophecies represents the deep mind at work without immediate reference to the continuities of workaday life.

The success of the late poems as forms of religious art is achieved in another way. Almost always clear in their broad meaning, and no less psychological than the *Songs,* they are sometimes less accessible in their particulars and especially in the relationship to each other of those particulars. Though I have no intention of trying to read the prophecies here, I shall try to point out several connections between them and the *Songs,* clustering most of my observations around two topics, the mind and sexuality. Both subjects are not only common to *Songs* and prophecies alike but crucial to them. Both reveal the appropriateness of bringing a knowledge of redemption derived from the *Songs* to bear in a reading of the prophetic works.

We may come to realize (as chimney sweepers, say) that we must acknowledge and not rationalize the threat of death. And subsequent to our understanding, we may in some degree face death and annihilate our false selves. But if Albion/Christ, the One Man towards Whom we direct all our spiritual motion, is made to acknowledge the fact of death and then to die, what are we to understand about our individual obligation to do so?[1] As I have implied in the previous chapter, the question is a version of the old theological question: works or grace, man's will or God's? As I have also implied, Blake complicates an already difficult question not by answering in favor of one or the other, as Spenser and Fielding, for instance, were moved to do, but in favor of both and neither.

In trying to explain the relationship between individual and universal entities, Damrosch cites Nicholas of Cusa as a likely source for Blake's view: " 'In each individual the universe is by contraction . . . what the particular individual is; and every individual in the universe is the universe, though the universe is in each individual in a different way and each thing is in the universe in a different way.' With this literal and complete interpenetration of microcosm and macrocosm [Damrosch comments], Cusanus seeks . . . to show that although universals exist only in particulars, the particulars in turn exist in an ultimate order that subsumes them and gives them life."[2] Though Cusa's formulation seems right, it also seems to *require* the mutuality it claims, not to *discover* or *reveal* it. Philosophically speaking, he invents "universal" simply by calling it the implicit sum of individuals. Instead of an abstraction to represent the relationship between individual and universal identities, we may prefer a sense of the dynamic connections between the two, even at the risk of lessening their stability as categories. Blake seems to me to invite us both to build and dissolve such categories.

William Dennis Horn, in an engaging article on Blake's treatment of the self, identifies the recognition of eternal being beyond Selfhood as the recognition that we have no temporal self, and further identifies it as the recognition that we have no *nontemporal* self. But the nature of the movement beyond Selfhood apparently understood by Horn renders the term "nontemporal self" inappropriate. To be fair, I should say that Horn may be relying as much on the history of philosophical and critical treatment of the self from Descartes to Bloom as he is on Blake for his view that "the problems raised by Freud's tendency to postulate a substantive unconscious are paradigmatic of all [fallacious] attempts to identify a central self."[3] Nevertheless, it seems to me that for Blake any experience that gets one beyond Selfhood leaves one with an individual identity whose attributes include a sense of its continuity with universal humanity. If we are beyond temporal self, we are poised both to *become* the One Man or universal humanity, and to *recognize* our individual affinity with him. In the *becoming,* we may be said to have neither temporal nor nontemporal self. But in the *recognition,* we operate out of a center that is uniquely our own, at least in the sense that it is continuous with earlier recognitions out of that same center. One might further argue that the more complete the recognitions, the more complete one's becoming the universal humanity, the ultimate implication of "completeness" being that the recognizing faculty would never be required again. On this view, *being* universal humanity and *recognizing* that we have become it would be categories separable by language, but also categories that dissolve and merge into each other in the ultimate event. The prophecies, however, do not bear out the argument. The fall, which these works characterize extensively, no less than the redemption towards which they direct their great actions, is inherent in eternity. The Zoas and their emanations may reunite in Albion, and in fact they do. But the division that is the fall, and that accounts at least for the present state of our individuality, is everlastingly potential: "Individual Identities never change nor cease."[4]

Though we seem required by the text to understand that even the most liberated of the speakers in *Songs of Experience* continues to live in the fallen world at one level of being, it may be reasonable to view some of them briefly again, with an eye for evidence of their movement beyond Selfhood and even beyond their individual identities. The speaker of "The Human Abstract" elaborates the human brain's unconscious fondness for nurturing the Tree of Mystery, and in so doing, he not only marks the nature of the mind's fallen condition, he also eliminates the distinction between one mind and all minds—he consolidates their geographies. The speaker of "London" both sees and hears, everywhere, the evidence of humanity's "mind-forg'd manacles," and he imagines their already ubiquitous hold extended over time, through the generations, by "Marriage hearse." Not only does the speaker of "A Poison Tree" exceed the limit of his old morality, he also locates—he relocates—the action of his conflict in the world of mind, into which he draws his foe in defiance of "external reality." The speaker of "The Tyger" finds the forests of the night to be continuous with the mind of God, and the discovery both enlarges his earlier limited world and frees him to redefine the Creator and their relationship to each other. In his explicit recognition that the shadow of thwarted sexuality has a deadly power, the speaker of "The Sick Rose" makes the inner world of the mind the determinant of the outer world of our natural lives. At one level of action, the speaker of "The Fly" moves through the portals of his mind from self, to fly, to butterfly, to eternity. The speaker of "To Tirzah" is blessed with a breathtaking economy of vision that joins four categories of experience—he sees that his own sexual, death-bound history and the history of fallen humanity are one and the same, and he sees that the death of one man, Jesus, is his own and the world's salvation.

The psychological movement from self to loss of temporal self, and from individual to universal being—at least from some nominally finite experience to its much larger imaginative implications—is characteristic of these songs. Later in Blake's work, the second territory of this movement, the world to which the visionary mind has traveled becomes the setting of the prophecies. This opening of the single mind into some aspect of the manifold mind, without immediate contradiction from the limits of conventional categories, is not peculiar to Blake among the romantics. Wordsworth, Coleridge, Shelley, and Keats all make good use of just such imaginative control of perceptual continuities. But they are unlike Blake in that one way or another they qualify the eternal vision with natural aftermath. Wordsworth's philosophic mind, however valuable to imagination, reincorporates death into its vision, modifying the glory and the freshness of the dream. Coleridge's Ancient Mariner has experienced a transforming vision of life in death, but he returns to his first home, where he seems unable to reorganize the natural world significantly, either for himself or others.[5] Though Keats's Endymion is transformed in a way that would have pleased

Blake—transformed until, at one level of perception, he can no longer distinguish between earth's Indian Maid and immortality's Cynthia—Keats himself seems to have set aside this capacity for making the natural world and eternity continuous with each other in favor of the moving ambivalences of the great odes, which toll him back to his sole self, unless the Hyperion fragments represent the late survival of Endymion's vision in the young poet.[6] Shelley opens the representative mind of Prometheus so that it becomes the whole universe, and in "The Sensitive Plant" the natural man's view of the seasonal round is shaken if not displaced by the speaker's counterview, made on behalf of eternity. But despite these and similar continuities between individual and universal perspectives in Shelley's poetry, it elsewhere expresses serious doubts about such continuities, in *Alastor,* "Hymn to Intellectual Beauty," *Julian and Maddalo,* and *The Triumph of Life.* Probably Stuart Curran is right to claim that Shelley is not inconsistent in this regard but honest in exploring the full range of possibility.[7] If so, one might say about Shelley's vision of the continuity between the world's individuals and eternity that it does not include a contrary aftermath, it simply occupies a place among Shelley's alternative visions.

Unlike the poems of visionary continuity of his fellow romantics, Blake's do not include a qualifying aftermath in individual poems. Nor are they located in a qualifying context of other poems by him, expressing an alternative vision. The vectors between individual and universal, this world and eternity, all point one way. By the end of the poem, I recognize fatigue and perplexity in the speaker of "The Tyger," and I understand that he is still in one sense in the natural world, but I cannot imagine that he will turn back from his discovery. Having broken through the limits of their individual perceptions to a larger world beyond, Blake's characters impress one as engaged in a "forward" motion, however painful the journey. The speakers of "London," "The Human Abstract," and "The Sick Rose," no less than the speaker of "To Tirzah," move into larger worlds of perception than their private lives require, and they seem never to return. In psychologically related movements outward by speakers in Wordsworth's poems—"Tintern Abbey," "The Solitary Reaper," the Immortality Ode—there is a pleasure of sad repose that epitomizes the best moment of the experience, available to recollection "forever," but there is also a return to the natural world of individual being. Keats's odes are similar in this regard, as are Coleridge's conversation poems. I have no wish to reduce these admittedly complicated works of the other romantics to just one thing. My point is that Blake's characters are unusual, perhaps unique, in that the journey out, from individual to the universe beyond, is uncomplicated by residual affinity for the world departed.

For all their passion of response to the world they break out of, Blake's characters never look back once they have broken out. They look ahead to the larger world they have discovered. They often continue to face difficulties in their new psychic "locations," but they do not return or try to return or think of trying to return to their starting point. The exception is Thel, the character without a Selfhood, who inevitably turns away from experience. All the others either make unconscious use of Selfhood as the instrument of their self-deception and remain tied to the natural world of experience as the only life, or they recognize the tight control on their vision exercised by Selfhood and endure the dislocation that attends the recognition. Consider the Wordsworth of the Immortality Ode or the Keats of the great odes in this regard. Their speakers seem to go out past Selfhood to a point at which their individual being is at liberty to join some order of the universe beyond it; indeed, the two become one. Wordsworth's speaker rejoins the everlasting infant seer in all of us, that best philosopher, trailing clouds of glory. And Keats's speaker of "Ode to a Nightingale" joins the bird of eternity who has always sung, darkling, in some melodious plot, exempted from the fate of hungry generations. But neither speaker permanently exceeds the bounds of self, identified by Wordsworth as the aging natural man, and by Keats as the abiding self-consciousness attuned to the terminal sound of the tolling bell. The aesthetic resolution, in these and many other romantic poems, includes a return. It seems to imply that the imagination's discovery or invention of eternal life includes a deep recognition of death, which enriches the whole experience of life. In such poems, death is not only the psychological barrier (Selfhood) between individual and eternal being, it is also an irrevocable fact to which the imagination must accede very shortly after it has moved from individual to universal experience. The whole adventure will have enlarged life significantly, but it will not finally have reduced death. For the very perception of death as an ally that deepens the sense of life is an acknowledgement that it is also the last reality.

For Blake, individual self or being or identity, once expanded beyond itself, does not contract. At least, that is the conclusion that accords with the psychology of Blake's characters in the *Songs*. They will not have been liberated from Selfhood so absolutely as to be in eternity. That is not the point. Think of the fatigue and uncertainty of "The Tyger's" speaker and the state of other liberated speakers by the time their statements end. For all their visionary control of new truths, these characters are left to grapple with the natural world. But once their journey has begun, nothing in their psychology is comparable to the accommodation of death one finds in poems by other romantics. It is as if the first part of the journey out has implicitly identified both the world (or state) they will depart and the world they will seek. Equally important, the identification is not qualified by doubts as to the value of the journey.

We know from songs like "The Little Black Boy," "The Chimney Sweeper," and "The Sick Rose" that Selfhood is deeply fastened to individual identity, manipulating it unscrupulously with great strength and ingenuity. And we know from *The Book of Thel* that its basis is the threat of death in the natural world, absolutely unbearable unless first rationalized by Selfhood. The combination implies that any movement of individual self from the control of Selfhood can be accomplished only at great emotional cost, and in fact we have seen that it is so in more than a few of the *Songs of Experience*. We are now in a position to consider that the experience of these characters making new discoveries includes not only their recognition of death, which Thel could not bear, but their nonregressive recognition.

It is plausible to suppose that a universal psychological characteristic assigned by Blake to all his speakers engaged in redemptive activity may very well be a part of Blake's own psychology or the psychology he would like to be his own. If so, one may regard the nonregressive recognition of death among Blake's speakers as a reflection of his preferred way of looking at things. Though the full enlargement of individual into eternal being is a labor never to be completed by mortals, the way between the two, once glimpsed, can never be doubted; and the enemy, under one psychological disguise or another, is to be sought everywhere. Taken as a whole, *Songs of Innocence and of Experience* may be regarded as the individuated prelude to the prophecies, whose setting is the universal mind. In one sense, of course, it is to us, his readers, that he displays the relatively simple intense outline of his redemptive process in the *Songs*. But he also discovers it there for himself. Having glimpsed eternity and the barrier to it from his studies of individual perception—first confined by Selfhood and then liberated from it in some important degree—he goes on with his religious anatomy, exploring the unlimited topography of the universal mind. At some point along the way, as if to express explicit confirmation of the connection between the two orders of his work, and between the two orders of the human mind as well, he revisits the *Songs*, by 1805 or so. That is, in "To Tirzah," his speaker uses the language of individual perception to lay out the subject of the prophecies, the history of the lost continuity between individual and universal mind (the fall). He argues there that the fall is a consequence of a flawed generative relationship between death and sexuality; of the incapacity of the mind to grasp the fact of that flawed relationship; and finally of the perpetuation of that incapacity by Tirzah, the mother of our mortal part. He also reveals his painful and angry discovery of the imposition, including its history and his conviction that for him the death of Jesus has broken the hold our bound senses have on our minds.

The biographical view I offer here may be too symmetrical, but to the extent that it is sound, there emerges from it Blake's idea of individual identity as a strong organizing sensibility, conscious of itself after the reduction of Selfhood's control over it, living in accordance with its conviction that it has to explore itself so that it may ultimately realize the totality of being. Even without the biographical model to support it, the idea may be inferred with assurance from the *Songs* alone, whether or not one includes "To Tirzah," once the psychological nature and power of Selfhood are understood. The strength required for such psychological movement—its recognition and acceptance of painful truth about its past, its purposive and essentially impersonal direction, its belief in its kinship with other minds—presupposes such an idea of individual identity. Indeed, the unusual intensity of many of the *Songs of Experience* might seem excessive if it were not traceable to just such a difficult continuity—a religiously endowed consciousness turning passionately away from Selfhood and passionately towards what it recognizes as its ultimate manifestation, complete humanity.

It is this intensity that displaces, if it does not invalidate, the question about grace or works, predestination or free will. Blake's poetry assumes our common humanity and catches us up, or works to catch us up, in the process of discovering that humanity, which given its eternally dynamic nature has no being distinct from the process. In such a context, a choice between grace and works is empty, because such choice derives from quite another level of mental life. Accordingly, the relevant issue for us as Blake's readers is *perception* of the process, which becomes *participation* in it, if we are sufficiently moved by Blake's intensity. I believe the *Songs* and *Thel,* more than the prophecies, are likely to help us in this regard.

It may seem a paradox that Blake refers to death much more directly and much more often in the prophecies than in the *Songs,* while the sense of

real risk to life seems less in the prophecies than in the *Songs*.[8] The threat
of death, on which deliverance from Selfhood, of course, continues to turn
in the prophecies, is attenuated by their special context, a universe in
which body, death's object, is variously but consistently treated as a func-
tion of mind. Terrible things happen to apparently human anatomies there,
but they happen in a flux of events that often dissipates sympathy, unless
one carries a deeply felt sense of the experience of Self-annihilation to the
long poems. Death is occasionally potent for more than a moment in the
prophecies, so that, as readers, we have room enough to identify ourselves
with death's victims, as for example in Vala's lament for her murder of
Albion:

My Father gave to me command to murder Albion
In unreviving Death; my Love, my Luvah orderd me in night
To murder Albion the King of Men. he fought in battles fierce
He conquerd Luvah my beloved: he took me and my Father
He slew them: I revived them to life in my warm bosom
He saw them issue from my bosom, dark in Jealousy
He burnd before me: Luvah framd the Knife & Luvah gave
The Knife into his daughters hand! such thing was never known
Before in Albions land, that one should die a death never to be reviv'd!
For in our battles we the Slain men view with pity and love:
We soon revive them in the secret of our tabernacles. . . .[9]

Or identified as irrevocable, death may seem momentarily threatening:
"Los & Enitharmon builded Jerusalem weeping / . . . Terrified at Non Exis-
tence / For such they deemd the death of the body."[10] But the whole mode
and subject matter of the prophecies are a fulfillment of the spiritual axiom
that "When the mortal disappears in improved knowledge cast away / The
former things so shall the Mortal gently fade away / And so become invisi-
ble to those who still remain."[11] In Blake's long poems death is to be
regarded as one of the former things, seen through the medium of an
improved knowledge.

In the *Songs of Experience,* on the contrary, characters are moved slowly
towards a recognition of death's constraints upon them, and we see what
they see and the anguish it costs them. We participate in the beginnings of
their redemption, which may thus become our own. Though characters in
the prophecies may also move slowly to the recognition that death is
responsible for their satanic Selfhood—Milton does, for instance—the

poem, which includes a clearer vision of the matter than theirs, implies their deliverance to us long before it is effected. We remember the Song of the Bard and the salvation it sponsors. We may be moved by the mythologized figure of Milton as he faces Self-annihilation, but he is not likely to engage us as much in consciousness as do the readily identifiable human characters of the early poems. In the informed context of the prophecies, death is too well known and too well understood to be deeply threatening. One result of this knowledge is that death is named "Death" there, not, for example "the poison of a smile" or "a thousand fighting men in ambush." It is also identified there as the arch-inhibitor of immortal life, flourishing only in the natural world, or as the imagination's instrument for freeing itself from Selfhood—Self-annihilation. In short, the natural power of death there has yielded almost completely to the power of mental life.

It is a measure of Blake's spiritual maturing that the sense of death has been transformed in this by no means unqualified way from early to late works. Where it may exist, any distance between ourselves and him in this regard suggests a value in carrying the intensity of his early treatment of the matter with us to the prophecies. He obviously carried it with him, in some assimilated form, which includes the recognition that the vision of individual identity beyond Selfhood is nonregressive and continuous with the full divine humanity. Without a comparable sense of death, we may, despite ourselves, read the prophecies too neutrally.

Along with the treatment of individual mind becoming universal mind after bringing Selfhood across the threshold of death, it is the treatment of sexuality that most clearly displays Blake's unwavering psychological regard of things in the movement from *Songs* to prophecies. But other subjects reveal it too. His exploration of the full mental life in the prophecies, from the perspective of mind partially liberated from the control of Selfhood, may be clarified by a look at some of them. By the time the *Songs* end, several characters have experienced profound recognitions, and one knows or infers that they have experienced psychological reorientations as well. Though in their labors of perception they have penetrated deeply beneath the world's social surfaces and the individual mind's rationalizing shields, they have not grappled with fundamental questions. Why is the world a place of hostility and destruction rather than a place of love and forgiveness? Why at a certain moment did the sexes spring from shame and pride? Why does a tree of mystery grow in the human brain? These questions about evil or nominal evil may baffle characters who come close to them in the *Songs,* but no real effort is made to answer them, except by the speaker of "To Tirzah," and his answer is cryptic, far from clear. Having used the lyric with great success to do things it had never done before, Blake might have used it to include an adequately full genesis of the state of fallen humanity. But the Bard's "Introduction" to *Songs of Experience* and "Earth's Answer," with "To Tirzah" and one or two other poems, identify the relatively confined expression of his interest in the subject in the *Songs*. On the other hand, it is a subject very much in his way in these early poems. It is also one of the subjects he treats most fully in *The Four Zoas, Milton,* and *Jerusalem.*

If we consider Blake the poet's movement, we see in the *Songs* a surprisingly curtailed treatment of the origins of Earth's predicament, and in the prophecies an expansive treatment of the same subject. But there is sameness as well as difference in the movement from early to late works. Blake avoids issues of theodicy in both. Questions of the sort that might be taken to register a sense of universal injustice in the *Songs* are not considered there in moral terms. For example the question in "The Tyger"—"Did he who made the Lamb make thee?"—is made to imply that the speaker's notions of Creator and created need redefining rather than that God's goodness needs justification. Just so, Blake's vision of the fall in the long poems is essentially psychological. This continuity is important for reaffirming the center of Blake's interest, mental processes, rather than some system of acts, preferred and proscribed. The prophecies not only continue but enlarge this commitment to displaying the universe of psychological forces in motion rather than in explaining them in moral terms.[12] In fact, the fall in the prophecies is a psychological dislocation of the eternal mind owing not to a transgression, but to a possibility inherent in the mind's dynamics, which constitute a system of such magnitude and complexity as to exclude nothing. The complete context of being and event in the prophecies—the mind as the whole world—is another expression of Blake's view that mental things are alone real and that we must look into ourselves for a knowledge of the fall and into ourselves for redemption.

> . . . Los grew furious raging: Why stand we here trembling around
> Calling on God for help; and not ourselves in whom God dwells
> Stretching a hand to save the falling Man.[13]

As he charts the interior world of the prophecies, Blake does not turn away from social elements of the sort he identifies in "London," "The Little Black Boy," and the two versions of "The Chimney Sweeper" and "Holy

Thursday." That is, we encounter in the long poems not only the imperious personifications of mental attributes like Urizen, Palamabron, and their Emanations, not only the Eternals and Jesus, all of whom might be thought to have a place in that interior geography, but also such London places as South Molton Street and Stratford Place, and such persons from Blake's exterior life as Scofield and Kox. In *Jerusalem,* a personified London says,

> Return, Albion, return! I give myself for thee:
> My streets are my, Ideas of Imagination.
> Awake Albion, awake! And let us awake up together.
> My Houses are Thoughts: my Inhabitants; Affections,
> The children of my thoughts, walking within my blood-vessels.[14]

Blake carries social life into the whole universe of the mind, implying that its functional reality is located there and that its terrible features can be renovated only there. Persons, too, nominally outside, are incorporated into the universe of mind, in a similar continuity of subject and object.

> We live as One Man; for contracting our infinite senses
> We behold multitude; or expanding: we behold as one,
> As One Man all the Universal Family.[15]

The *Songs* presuppose the ultimate rightness of such continuity between subject and object, one being and another. For example, the Bard's "O Earth O Earth return!" and "Why wilt though turn away" imply the ideal of union between Word and Flesh, Eternity and created world, female and male, in *Songs of Experience. Songs of Innocence* implies the same ideal, most obviously, perhaps, through the identification of lamb, Christ, child, and speaker in "The Lamb." But the idea of the external world as intractably natural in appearance, with its discrete persons and objects and systems, is given a prominent place in the *Songs,* however qualified that place. By contrast, the prophecies stress the natural world's dependence on eternity. It is a world whose history is the history of the fall from eternity, and a world whose beings are separate from each other as a result of the fall. Accordingly, in the prophecies, recognitions of the mutuality of being are movements "upward" from the fall, and they are typically characterized without explanation. Jesus in one of His aspects may be indistinguishable from Los, and in another, indistinguishable from Luvah.[16] But in the *Songs* the recognition of such mutuality occasions surprise or wonder. The recognition is qualified by the lingering sense that it is a function of privileged or anomalous perception. Of course, the speaker of "The Fly" is a fly. But he is also, of course, a man. Beyond the spiritually invigorating tension between these two views, there is a sense in which they are opposed realities. One is imaginative and one is worldly. Not so, or much less so, in the prophecies. There, Blake's incorporation of the natural into the eternal subverts the possibility of such spiritual implications in physical things.

Closely related, sometimes concomitant with his treatment of subject and object, is Blake's treatment of time and space, which in the prophecies undermines the reader's sense of the natural world. Blake cannot represent the complex action of *Milton* as he might like, in a single arterial pulse, because his language relies on sequence for its representation. The same limitation makes it impossible for the simultaneous descents of Milton and Ololon to be represented to us simultaneously in the poem, as they could be in a painting.[17] And the representation of characters implies space; they are inevitably assigned to locations, if not to bodies with well-defined shapes, and they are reported as performing actions. Nevertheless, Blake modifies the conventional ideas of time and space in the prophecies by disregarding or violating the continuities and relationships they are generally understood to imply. He also subordinates time and space to the eternal mind, which in its fall requires them as a protection against "eternal torment."[18] Though "not one Moment / Of Time is lost, nor one Event of Space unpermanent / . . . all remain . . . [so that] The generations of men run on in the tide of Time / But leave their destind lineaments permanent for ever & ever";[19] time and space "vary according as the Organs of Perception vary."[20] They also come to an end.

It is true that the *Songs* point the way to such liberty, but they are much more plainly ambivalent than the prophecies, leaving the reader to weigh the contrast between freedom from time and place on the one side, and their remorselessness as conditions of the natural world on the other. The Bard of the Introduction to *Songs of Experience* "Present, Past, & Future sees." Laughter in "Laughing Song" makes woods, stream, air, hill, meadows, grasshopper, Mary, Susan, Emily, painted birds, and the speaker one continuous space. Laughter also replaces time by making the "sweet chorus of Ha, Ha, He" the interminable sound of life. One could easily add to these instances; the point remains that the *Songs* do not typically deliver even their most visionary characters entirely from their sense for temporal and spacial controls. Even the speaker of "To Tirzah" continues to be caught up by the exigencies of the natural world, thinking of himself intensely as he does in the terms of his bound senses.

It is not that such a speaker's vision is regressive in the least but that we encounter him at the turning point, where his discovery is characterized in terms that remind us of ourselves. We feel a special kinship with the worldly side of his experience. The psychological power of his transforming moment from Selfhood to individual identity prepares us to experience the power of the prophecies. Entered directly, the prophecies may show us little we recognize in the blood and along the heart, so clearly do they subordinate the natural world to eternity or represent its actions in psychological terms that we may ponder to abstraction. But if we enter them through the passage of the *Songs,* we share their pathos. Having become the son of Tirzah at the moment he begins to see that he is Jesus, just as we have become the man who joins the fly within and beyond himself, and as we have become that other man who passes through the dark barrier between himself and the Tyger, we are prepared to feel the human force of the prophecies.

The sexuality of the *Songs* also continues in a changed form in the prophecies. In populating the world of the long poems with characters who are defined in the terms of complex sexuality, and in showing them to be almost hopelessly divided from each other and in deep need of each other, in a flux of sexual preoccupations and actions, Blake both extends his treatment of sexuality in the *Songs* and gives it a new prominence.

In *Songs of Experience,* Bard and Earth are sexually inclusive characters who represent us all. Their dialogue tells us that the Word needs flesh, the imagination needs sexuality, sexuality needs liberty, the fallen world has reduced sexuality and as a result has constrained imagination. In short, Bard and Earth represent the state of the world fallen from Eternity, and they represent the possibility of redemption too, in their ultimate union. Their poems, "Introduction" and "Earth's Answer," anticipate many of the important experiences of characters in both *Songs* and prophecies. But in reading even the songs that quickly follow these first two *Songs of Experience,* we may not always remember their early message, that biology qualifies every aspiration of the spirit. Though we meet characters in the *Songs* whose sexuality may be understood to fulfill the expectations aroused by Bard and Earth, they are likely to interest us as highly individual persons with histories of their own. In this regard, I think especially of the Nurse of Experience, the maiden Queen, the Sick Rose, the Youth and pale Virgin, and Ona.

Grounded as they are on a mortality we recognize as our own, their experiences are available to us emotionally. At one level it hardly matters that we may be less troubled sexually than they. Or that many readers may be males, whereas most of these characters are Earth's daughters. What Thel rejected, we and they must confront, whether we are men or women, whether or not we appear to be more fortunate than they are. But the more deeply we respond to these characters individually, the more keenly we feel our response to be to the particular experience they represent.

As if to guard against this separation of individual sexual predicament from the general fallen state of sexuality, Blake disperses throughout the prophecies the idea represented in *Songs of Experience* by the division of Bard from Earth. In the long poems the idea is represented by a vast proliferation of sexual divisions, male from female, among the fragmented psychological elements of the complete humanity. The chief implication of the Bard's "Introduction" (*Songs*), that sexuality is universally a vital element of the mind, is amplified in the prophecies, primarily in that mental life itself, the whole geography of the later poems, is shown to be organized along sexual lines. That world is filled with actively sexual beings, derivatives of the fragmented mind, whose states are represented as persons flowing into and out of each other, in keeping with their sexual need and activity. That world identifies spiritual loss and gain in sexual terms more extensively than in the terms of labor or knowledge. Finally, it often represents the very progression from fallen state to nonnatural eternity as arising from a sexual relationship.

This largely sexual organization of the totality of being and action is only incidentally a reflection of the fall. True, sexuality derives from the mind. "The Treasures of Heaven are ... Realities of Intellect from which All the Passions Emanate."[21] And sexuality will finally be returned to Intellect. But these are formulations for understanding relationships rather than for fixing a hierarchy. In the dynamics of psychological process, sexuality is a constrained or fulfilled potentiality, not only for physical intercourse, but for all human commingling and for cooperative endeavor generally.[22] It is the promise that we may exceed ourselves and join others in imaginatively enlarging union. It is, or it generates, the capacity to forgive. It is Jesus in us, without the fear of death that requires self-defense, self-deception, hatred, and constraint. One would not exaggerate the place Blake gives it by saying that sexuality is the power that informs the mind's systems. We love, hope, hate, fear, aspire, labor, and despair, using sexually informed energies. But in spite of its full and prominent location throughout the prophecies, Blake seems to have had some doubt as to our capacity to understand that each of us experiences most of life in the meanings of this sexual abundance:

> Men understand not the distress & the labour & sorrow
> That in the Interior Worlds is carried on in fear & trembling
> Weaving the shuddring fears & loves of Albions Families.[23]

Beyond the radical and extensive distribution of sexuality in the world of the prophecies, Blake gives it a dramatic prominence in narrative incident, by presenting characters in intensely defined circumstances. Though he seems to me to guard against our seeing these characters in isolation, as I believe we typically see characters in the *Songs,* the episodic disjunction of the long poems may lead the reader to admire certain moments of sexual expressiveness, and to be attracted to them as isolable pieces. Vala's lament, already quoted, is an example. A further incentive to such isolation of characters is that even though they are, with few exceptions in the prophecies, personified aspects of mind and therefore recognizable as manifestations of humanity, they are also strangers to us, simply because of their psychologically special reason for being. One way of overcoming the nonnatural heritage of these characters is to extract them from the mental context in which they have been deliberately located and to think and feel about them as if they were human beings. In fact, such a response to them may be helpful, but only within limits. Among the many characters who for one reason or another may seem to invite such isolating regard is Oothoon as she makes her lyric speech "to the bright Marygold of Leutha's vale";[24] the Shadowy Female, in *Milton,* who "howls in articulate howlings";[25] and Mary and Joseph, whose story is told by the Divine Voice to Jerusalem.[26] But in fact all these and other such character-centered episodes include important links to the poetical context in which they occur. Characters may emerge momentarily from that context, but they are never free of it. If we as readers succeed in isolating them from their surroundings with one part of our minds, we are likely to do so having recognized the richness of the whole with another. This dual power of the text seems to me well exemplified in many of the monologues.

The graphic one that follows is typically connected with what comes before and after it, more by internal textual bonds than by the palpable opening and closing transitions.

Vala replied in clouds of tears Albions garment embracing

I was a City & Temple built by Albions children.
I was a Garden planted with beauty I allured on hill & valley
The River of Life to flow against my walls & among my trees
Vala was Albions Bride & Wife in great Eternity
The loveliest of the daughters of Eternity when in day-break
I emanated from Luvah over the Towers of Jerusalem
And in her Courts among her little Children offering up
The Sacrifice of fanatic love! Why loved I Jerusalem!
Why was I one with her embracing in the Vision of Jesus
Wherefore did I loving create love, which never yet
Immingled God & Man, when thou & I, hid the Divine Vision
In a cloud of secret gloom which behold involve me round about
Know me now Albion: look upon me I alone am Beauty
The Imaginative Human Form is but a breathing of Vala
I breathe him forth into the Heaven from my secret Cave
Born of the Woman to obey the Woman O Albion the mighty
For the Divine appearance is Brotherhood, but I am Love
Elevate into the Region of Brotherhood with my red fires[.]

Art thou Vala? replied Albion.[27]

Many images in the passage are easily pictorialized by the mind's eye—
"The River of Life [flows] against my walls," "I emanated from Luvah over
the Towers of Jerusalem," "Albion: look upon me [,] I alone am Beauty," "I
breathe [the Human Form] forth into the Heaven from my secret Cave," "I
am Love/Elevate . . . with my red fires." The passage also carries a host of
complex narrative signals. They are important in themselves and they
resonate with our already heightened sense that Albion's being is almost
hopelessly divided; he has exiled his emanation Jerusalem to "impalpable
voidness," and he is about to abstract from his own mind and to deify the
"Prince of Light," Urizen, as God.[28] These divisions and externalizations
include Vala and Luvah, whose emanation, of course, she is. Their loss to
Albion represents his utter confusion of emotional life. He goes so far as to
believe that it has some purpose entirely separate from himself. Having
grasped this idea of Albion's fall as a division and externalization of the
parts of his being, we may read Vala's speech as a confirmation of our
knowledge of his state—her affinity with multiplex aspects of created
things, her former place in eternity, her early love for Jerusalem, her

distorted claims about the relationship between God and Man and about her place in the human imagination, her connection with Jesus, her self-deception and destructiveness, her seductive and imperious sexuality.

In the prophecies, then, Blake takes the view of sexuality implicit in the dialogue between Bard and Earth—its fallen state and its importance for redemption—and he amplifies it, showing it to permeate the whole universe of mind. Built into the very fabric of the prophecies and not confined to one aspect of them, sexuality must be seen as exercising an unremitting psychological force in the complete humanity, however various its manifestations from one individual being to another. Moreover, the characterization of individual beings in sexual terms in the prophecies include many devices for relating them to the larger universe of which they are a part. Blake may be supposed thus to have overcome in the prophecies any potential discontinuity of the sort I have hypothesized between the first two poems of *Songs of Experience*—the dialogue between Bard and Earth about sexuality's fallen state and its importance to the redemption of the entire world—and the succeeding poems about Earth's daughters, whom we may regard too much as individual cases and too little as illustrations of fallen humanity's universal predicament. And yet he continues to doubt that he is understood: "Men understand not the . . . / . . . loves of Albions Families." Why should he doubt?

It might be argued that Blake, believing he had not well enough kept alive in the reader's mind the universal significance of sexuality in the songs about Earth's daughters, took care in the prophecies to stress that universality by the very mode of his poetry. Unfortunately (the argument might continue), as a result of this choice of mode, he lost the power to engage the reader as he had in the *Songs,* by means of a close identification with characters. His doubts, then, might be explained as the result of some lingering sense of inadequacy about his treatment of sexuality. But I wonder whether his doubt is about himself or about us. There is probably a good deal of truth in what I have suggested about the continuity with difference in the treatment of sexuality from *Songs* to prophecies and about what it implies for the reader. We identify ourselves closely with Earth's daughters, less with the idea represented by Bard and Earth. But I believe Blake's real concern is that "Men understand not." They are more intractable about sexuality than they are about any other subject, except death.

In the *Songs of Experience* and *The Book of Thel,* sexuality and death are closely identified with each other. Sexually constrained, pale Virgin and

Youth arise from their graves and aspire to death. The Sick Rose's dark
secret love "Does [her] life destroy." The Garden of Love is filled with
"graves, / And tomb-stones where flowers should be." "The Sexes sprung
from Shame & Pride / Blow'd in the morn: in evening died." And Thel
cannot distinguish between death and her emerging sexuality. Whether
constrained or whether contemplated from the perspective of desire, sexu-
ality is part of the consciousness of death in these early poems. One may
also find close associations between sexuality and death in the prophecies.
In *Milton,* Elynittria brings Leutha to Palamabron's bed, and Leutha "In
dreams ... bore the shadowy Spectre of Sleep, & namd him Death."[29] In
Jerusalem, Vala follows her father's "command to murder Albion / In
unreviving Death," an act that disconcerts her—"such thing was never
known / Before in Albion's land ... , / For in our battles we the Slain men
view with pity and love: / We soon revive them."[30] In *The Four Zoas,*
Tharmas tells us that "The Men have received their death wounds & their
Emanations are fled."[31] But whereas, with very few exceptions, death and
sexuality are perceived to be very like each other by characters in the early
poems, they are variably perceived in the major prophecies. There, as the
characters are renewed, sexuality ceases being "Sexual Love as iron
chains," sprung from "spiritual Hate."[32] Instead, it sponsors the recognition
of humanity's unity: "I am in you and you in me, mutual in love divine."[33]
And though it is true that the term "death" occurs with much greater
frequency in the major prophecies than in any other works by Blake, as a
glance at the concordance will show, it is, as I have already remarked,
attenuated by the very context in which it occurs, where mental and eternal
sponsorship implicitly redefines it as subordinate to life. We are left then
with this engaging relationship: sexuality, in the form of the power of love
to join us to each other, grows in the prophecies in something like an
inverse ratio to the lessening power of death.

The general Blakean answer to the question why death should be less
deadly in proportion as sexuality becomes more effective as an expression
of love is fairly clear. Death is frightening to the natural man, who fears it as
his utter terminus, and in that state of fear, though he regards sex as a
means of overcoming death, he also regards it as a *memento mori*—
probably, to judge from Thel, the equivalent of death itself at some deep
level of his mind. But as sexuality becomes increasingly a function, not of
Selfhood but of individual identity, it serves death less and imagination
more, giving us both our fullest selves and each other too. Selfhood's dying
is sexuality's deliverance.

As he journeys through the world of the mind in the prophecies, Blake is certain enough about individual identity and its continuity with universal humanity to display the nature of our sexual life apart from what death makes it in the unliberated imagination. It is not only that those who make love only to make children anticipate their own replacement—death—but also that the confinement of sexuality to biological purpose confirms Selfhood's domination of life and thus adds to the limiting power of death. Free of Selfhood, its functions multiplied, sexuality serves art and religion, finally, and in so doing, it both overcomes generation and exceeds its limits. It is no longer the servant of death.

Though the early poems do not, like the prophecies, illustrate this dynamic relationship between sexuality and death, they help us to understand it. It is not always specifically sexual repression that accounts for the formation of Selfhood, but it is always a repression in support of the mere compulsion to repeat generational life. We may forget momentarily, as we read about the Sick Rose or the maiden Queen, that she is a daughter of Earth, who inherits the fallen world the Bard longs for in its redeemed form. But we are not likely to miss her mortal need to grapple with the sexuality of death from which Thel ran shrieking. Without this knowledge, I do not believe the prophecies, for all their sexual amplitude and complexity, would be as accessible as Blake hoped they might be.

Notes

Chapter 1

1. Northrop Frye, "Blake's Introduction to Experience," in *Blake: A Collection of Critical Essays,* ed. Frye (Englewood Cliffs, N.J.: Prentice-Hall, 1966), provides a theoretical basis for this movement between *Songs* and the prophecies: "Actually Blake, however versatile, is rigorously consistent in both his theory and practice as an artist. . . . While he was working on the *Songs of Innocence and of Experience,* he was also working on their prophetic counterparts" (p. 23). Robert F. Gleckner, *The Piper and the Bard* (Detroit: Wayne State University Press, 1957), devotes a long opening section to Blake's whole vision of things before turning to the *Songs.* Harold Bloom, *Blake's Apocalypse* (Garden City, N.Y.: Doubleday, 1963), draws a line between *Songs of Experience* and "Blake's more ambitious and greater works" (p. 129), but the terms he uses for criticism of the *Songs* often derive from the other works—"Reprobate," "Elect," "Redeemed" (p. 131). Joseph H. Wicksteed, *Blake's Innocence and Experience* (New York: E. P. Dutton, 1928), is exceptional in trying to avoid what he knows about Blake's later works affect what he says about the *Songs:* "to elucidate early work by later . . . is a task to be undertaken with the utmost caution. It [is] necessary, therefore, to begin by making the *Songs* interpret the *Songs*" (p. 26). On the other hand, Wicksteed seems often to rely on terms deriving from orthodox Christianity for his commentary. In short, he too refers the *Songs* to a preestablished context for much of their meaning. I should point out that recently Gleckner, in *Blake's Prelude: "Poetical Sketches"* (Baltimore: The Johns Hopkins University Press, 1982), has provided a very different critical point of departure for reading the *Songs,* and he has done so without contradicting his earlier view:

One need not press . . . to recognize that in the *Introduction* to *Songs of Innocence* . . . a creator-singer-writer-artist-bookmaker is at work: the musician-creator (piper), the singer of words, the writer and (implicitly) maker of books—but books (as the final lines indicate) that are not only to be read but heard and "seen" in the same imaginative sense that the piper initially sees a child on a cloud. "Book" has become something other (or at least more) than an artifact "out there," the reader of which is merely a Lockean perceiver and understander of object. This other-than-artifact has not only imaginatively literalized the traditional "word-picture" idea of poetry but collapsed the senses, so to speak, into a wholeness of perception by which the "reader" can emulate the perceptive-creative act of the artist himself. (p. 155)

2. David Wagenknecht, *Blake's Night* (Cambridge, Mass.: Belknap Press of Harvard University Press, 1973), in fact treats all of Blake's work in the terms of pastoral, in very sophisticated readings. Zachary Leader, *Reading Blake's "Songs"* (London: Routledge & Kegan Paul, 1981), places the *Songs* in the context of this debate, but readings of individual poems are often based on'the psychology of Blake's characters, in part at least.

3. S. Foster Damon, *William Blake, His Philosophy and Symbols* (Gloucester, Mass.: Peter Smith, 1958; first published by Houghton Mifflin, 1924); Northrop Frye, *Fearful Symmetry* (Princeton, N.J.: Princeton University Press, 1947); Thomas R. Frosch, *The Awakening of Albion* (Ithaca, N.Y.: Cornell University Press, 1974); Susan Fox, *Poetic Form in Blake's "Milton"* (Princeton, N.J.: Princeton University Press, 1976); Christine Gallant, *Blake and the Assimilation of Chaos* (Princeton, N.J.: Princeton University Press, 1978).

4. David V. Erdman, Preface, *A Concordance to the Writings of William Blake,* 2 vols. (Ithaca, N.Y.: Cornell University Press, 1967), 1: vii.

5. Blake's freedom from morbidity and from other routine or conventional signs of response to death seems to operate not only in his poetry but in his pictorial art as well. Robert N. Essick, "Blake and the Traditions of Reproductive Engraving," in *The Visionary Hand,* ed. Essick (Los Angeles: Hennessey & Ingalls, 1973), provides a basis for this claim:

In the title-page to *Experience,* the shadows and folds at the foot of the bed, executed as masses rather than lines, have as firm a presence as the human figures and letters. This essentially sculptural conception of etching a plate in relief was very likely influenced by Blake's early experiences in Westminster Abbey, where he was sent by Basire to make sketches of the sepulchral monuments. Certainly the influence of tomb sculpture can be seen in the supine figures on the title-page to *Experience.* But whatever the sources for the motifs and style of Blake's relief etchings, they are not *reproductions;* they are the works-in-themselves, the final intentions of the artist unencumbered by a syntax foreign to their essential qualities. In the illuminated books, image and syntax are one. (p. 508)

All quotations of Blake's works are taken from *The Complete Poetry & Prose of William Blake,* rev. ed., ed. David V. Erdman (Berkeley and Los Angeles: University of California Press, 1982), unless otherwise noted.

6. David Hume, *Essays on the Immortality of the Soul* (London, 1783), appeared as *Essays on the Mortality of the Soul* (Edinburgh, 1789), a title closer than the original one to the spirit of the piece. Hume had died in 1776.

7. See, for example, *John Donne, Biathanotos,* reproduced from the First Edition, with a bibliographical note by J. Hebel (New York: Facsimile Text Society, 1930), where Donne raises such questions as whether death is evil (pp. 102–4) and says about suicide, "Whensoever any affliction assailes me, mee thinks I have the keyes of my prison in mine owne hand . . ." (p. 18); from *Songs and Sonets* to his last sermon, *Death's Duell* (1631), Donne was deeply concerned with the subject. In 1729, Swift made this admission: "I was 47 years old [in 1714] when I began to think of death; and the reflections upon it now begin when I wake in the Morning, and end when I go to sleep" (*The Correspondence of Jonathan Swift,* 5 vols., ed. Harold Williams [Oxford: Clarendon Press, 1963–65], 3:354). Boswell tells us, "The horrour of death which I had always observed in Dr. Johnson, appeared strong tonight [Tuesday, 16 September 1777; they had been discussing Hume's death]. . . . He said, 'he never had a moment in which death was not terrible to him' " (*Boswell's Life of Johnson,* 6 vols., ed. George Birkbeck Hill, rev. L. F. Powell [Oxford: Clarendon Press, 1934–50], 3:253).

8. Various Cambridge Platonists, deists and Shaftesburian moralists, for example, discovered a basis for natural religion in the perceptual relationship between the human observer and the physical world he occupied and thus renewed the endangered sense of continuity between this world and eternity. See Marjorie Hope Nicolson, *Mountain Gloom and Mountain Glory: The Development of the Aesthetics of the Infinite* (Ithaca, N.Y.: Cornell University Press, 1959); Ernest Lee Tuveson, *The Imagination as a Means of Grace* (Berkeley: University of California Press, 1960); Meyer H. Abrams, *Natural Supernaturalism* (New York: W. W. Norton, 1971). A culmination of the activity aimed at controlling life against death by philanthropic institutions was the Royal Humane Society, established to restore life to the apparently dead, chiefly the drowned. It had more than forty chapters in Great Britain, continental Europe, and the United States; George III was its patron. During the 1790s it is reported to have saved thousands of persons given up for dead. See *Gentlemen's Magazine,* 17:568–69. Its founder, William Hawes, implies much about the value he and his colleagues placed on their work: "To restore animation, is an act that seems to carry humanity beyond itself, and to approximate the divinity: as nothing can possibly exceed it but creation." *Royal Humane Society, Instituted 1774,* the annual report for 1790, p. 10. This and similar pamphlets about philanthropic organizations are gathered under one cover, named *Philanthropic and Humane Societies,* and given the Bodleian Library call number Gough London 37.

9. Christian mortalism is the view held by thousands of otherwise devout Christians in the seventeenth century (Milton was among them) that when we die our souls die too, or that our souls sleep until the Last Judgment, or that our souls

die until the Last Judgment. See Norman T. Burns, *Christian Mortalism* (Cambridge, Mass.: Harvard University Press, 1972).

10. Gleckner, for example, refers to "Blake's insistence that the shadow of experience constantly impinges upon the sunlit area of innocence" (p. 84). And E. D. Hirsch, Jr., *Innocence and Experience: An Introduction to Blake* (New Haven, Conn.: Yale University Press, 1964), says that "Innocence is a spiritual blessedness amid natural bleakness" (p. 31). Heather Glen, *Vision and Disenchantment: Blake's "Songs" and Wordsworth's "Lyrical Ballads"* (Cambridge: Cambridge University Press, 1983), having identified a dark side of *Songs of Innocence,* says these poems "do not dramatize a naively blinkered or partial point of view. The 'Divine Vision' of human *potentia* which they present is coherent and self-sufficient. And it is a vision that depends not on the denial of social realities Blake was elsewhere to confront, but on a careful poetic exploration of the interpenetration between ideal values and human experience within an actual society" (p. 111).

11. David V. Erdman, *The Illuminated Blake* (Garden City, N.Y.: Anchor Press/ Doubleday, 1974), for example, comments on one of the illustrations to "The Ecchoing Green" by saying, "two unplucked bunches of grapes are larger than the two plucked, the very largest . . . being perhaps just out of reach. But all these reachings can be managed in the world of innocent imagination in which vines are this sufficient and accommodating" (p. 48). Gleckner suggests a similar ease of connection between subject and object in Innocence: "unhindered communion between the child's life and the lives of animals and the surrounding universe" (p. 45). John Holloway, *Blake: The Lyric Poetry* (London: Edward Arnold, 1968), gives particular stress to this continuity of "inside" with "outside" by recording a series of identities in Innocence. In concluding his remarks on the Introduction to *Songs of Innocence,* he says, "There is no need now to tot up all the identities which compose the poem. Its manifold of equations issue from, and communicate, a world of harmonious oneness" (p. 62).

12. Here I do not take exception to the critical principle that it is important to keep the complexities of point of view in mind as we read the *Songs.* I wish only to concentrate for the moment on the child's perspective, without finally giving up the modifying perspectives of others, well identified, for instance, in Gleckner, pp. 64–66.

13. Bloom puts the matter this way: "By his own logic, [the Little Black Boy] ought to say that the English boy will be like himself at the last, but instead he gives us the opposite notion, the pathos of unfulfillable wish" (pp. 50–51). Leader says that the mother's lesson "has to compete [in the Little Black Boy's mind] with more deeply embedded presentiments of inferiority. He is glad that . . . he is God's favorite, but only because now the English child . . . will learn to love him" (p. 111).

14. In *Milton,* for example, the Bard's "Mark well my words! they are of your eternal salvation" is a statement implying the need for an "act of will." The voice that speaks "To the Public," prefatory to *Jerusalem,* seems to have Blake's authority when it says, "We who dwell on Earth can do nothing of ourselves, every thing is conducted by Spirits, no less than Digestion or Sleep." This statement implies that "acts of will" are impossible or useless. I happen to believe the two statements can be reconciled, but the point is that they seem to require reconciliation.

15. *Nineteenth-Century Accounts of William Blake,* ed. Joseph Anthony Wittreich, Jr. (Gainesville, Fla.: Scholars' Facsimiles & Reprints, 1970), p. 105.

16. Erdman, *The Complete Poetry and Prose of William Blake,* p. 674.

17. To what degree of completeness Self-annihilation may be brought has not proved a simple question. W. J. T. Mitchell, *Blake's Composite Art* (Princeton, N.J.: Princeton University Press, 1978), is unusual in saying flatly, " 'Self-annihilation' does not mean the permanent abolition of Selfhood; it is the prelude to the creation of a *new* Selfhood which will serve the imagination. Blake's rhetoric can be misleading on this point. His insistence on putting off the Selfhood 'always' (*Milton,* 40:36) and 'ever and ever' (*Milton,* 38:49) should be read in the sense of continuity, not finality" (p. 91n).

Most critics, like Frye and Bloom, seem to say that the vision of the mature artist-prophet is vision through the eye, without the interference of Selfhood. Such optimistic statements, however, seem to me to include a reservation or a doubt. Frye, *Fearful Symmetry,* for example, says, "the [visionary] artist does not wait to die before he lives in the spiritual world into which John [author of Revelation] was caught up" (p. 45). But the emphasis here is equivocal, I believe. Is Frye talking about the artist at the moment of his creative perception or about the artist as human being at just about any time in his life? Is salvation for the artist a moment's gift, which he may lose "forever," or lose for long periods of time, after blessed instances of his vision of eternity? Or does he move steadily to greater and greater illumination; and ultimately to eternity in this life "forever"? Bloom says, "the insistent argument of all Blake's poetry . . . is that the work of the creation by any artist of universal power and sympathy can clear away some encrustation from the natural creation and so demonstrate that the natural man is only an analogy of man" (p. 402). The word "some" heavily qualifies the chances of complete annihilation of the Selfhood, of course, and "demonstrate" raises questions about who is perceiving what and for how long.

It is really not surprising that the best among us should have enough understanding to believe that we might be able to clear ourselves of the heavy encrustation of the natural man and yet have doubts that we may do so. It seems appropriate to point out that E. D. Hirsch's view of Blake's psycho-spiritual development over the considerable period during which he composed the *Songs* provides a clear alternative to my sense that whatever Blake believes Eternity to be (the goal of Self-annihilation), he locates it primarily in the here and now, even though Eternity so located may be seldom or never available for most of us. Hirsch claims Blake was untypically "naturalistic" between 1790 and 1795, in the sense that he believed in a natural order which had been corrupted by priests and others in authority, and believed, too, that revolution in the physical world might restore the natural-divine. *Songs of Experience,* with the notable exception of "To Tirzah," are permeated by this naturalistic view and the optimism associated with it, Hirsch believes; "To Tirzah," added to the *Songs* no earlier than 1802, probably in 1805, marks Blake's return to a "primordial faith in Atonement, in the saving agencies of Mercy, Pity, Peace, and Love" (*Innocence and Experience,* p. 147). Hirsch's position, finally, is that for Blake, "the Last Judgment [one's Self-annihilation, is not only] an inner and visionary [event, but] a cosmological event [as well]" (p. 38). See also p. 92, n. 8.

Chapter 2

1. See, for example, Geshe Sopa, "Samathavipasyanayuganaddha: The Two Leading Principles of Buddhist Meditation," in *Mahayana Buddhist Meditation,* ed. Minoru 'Kiyota (Honolulu: The University Press of Hawaii, 1978), for this Buddhist view: "self is neither a *bona fide* phenomenon nor any other kind of actual or real [*sic*] and it is just this false apprehension of a self which is the ultimate basis or ground on which the [misleading] passions depend. Consequently the specifically Buddhist paths for the elimination of the passions are by way of removing this final ground of apprehension of a self through a direct perception of things as they in fact are, i.e., devoid of selfhood" (p. 57).

Though the syncretism that accounts for the coming together of Gnostic beliefs makes for considerable diversity, the idea of man as an eternal being, encrusted in a biological and biologically controlled body from which it must be liberated, is universal. "The dominant note in . . . [Gnostic] thought is that man is a divine being imprisoned in a mortal body" (R. M. Wilson, *The Gnostic Problem* [London: A. R. Mowbray, 1958], p. 258). W. C. van Unnik, *Newly Discovered Gnostic Writings,* trans. H. H. Hoskins (London: SCM Press, 1960), puts the matter this way: "Gnosticism wrestles for an understanding of the world and the self. . . . The true and essential being of Man belongs to and with the perfect God, but . . . finds itself situated in this imperfect world. . . . Through knowledge of himself and through awareness of his separation from God . . . Man must be set free from the tyranny of evil" (p. 22). Stuart Curran, "Blake and the Gnostic Hyle: A Double Negative," *Blake Studies,* 4, 2 (Spring 1972): 117–33, discriminatingly identifies similarities between Blake's work and Gnostic writings readily available to him; Curran also demonstrates Blake's rejection of the dualistic Gnostics, who repudiate matter because they are intimidated by it, assuring us that for Blake "nothing that seems material . . . cannot be humanized—spiritualized—when we see through, not with the eye" (p. 133).

A fairly conventional Christian view about the self to be done away with is represented by a change in translation from the King James to the Revised Standard Bible. The first gives, "our old man is crucified with [Christ], that the body of sin might be destroyed" (Romans 6:6); and the second gives for the same passage, "our old self was crucified with [Christ] so that the sinful body might be destroyed," to which is added the following gloss: "*The sinful body,* not the physical body as such, but the sinful self" (*The New Oxford Annotated Bible With the Apocrypha,* eds. Herbert G. May and Bruce M. Metzger [New York: Oxford University Press, 1973], p. 1367). A more unusual Christian identification of Selfhood and its annihilation, with interesting temporal overtones, was made by The Family of Love, a small Protestant sect founded in Holland by Hendrik Niclaes, who probably visited England about 1550. In *Terra Pacis. A True Testification of the Spiritual Lande of Peace, Which is the Spiritual Lande of Promyse . . .* (London? 1575?), Niclaes argues that every present moment contains past and future times. In order for one to perceive this eternity beyond time and mere circumstance, one must surrender to "Understanding" through the irrevocable abolition of "Selfnes"— "Despysing Self-Wills Choosing"—so that one may enter forever, in the here and now, not after death, "God's Holy Nature" (p. 82 left).

2. *Essais de Montaigne,* 2 vols, ed. Maurice Rat (Paris: Garnier Frères, 1974), 1: [1].

3. Frazer's *The Golden Bough,* 13 vols. (London: Macmillan, 1890–1936), has been corrected in many of its particulars and reduced to manageable proportions by various scholars. See, for example, *The New Golden Bough,* ed. Theodor H. Gaster (New York: Criterion Books, 1959). Both the corrections and the reductions are a tribute to the continuing vitality and influence of Frazer's work. Ceremonial acts that represent a movement in status, say from youth to adulthood, as symbolic death and rebirth, are a chief interest of van Gennep's *The Rites of Passage,* trans. Monika B. Vizedom and Gabrille L. Caffee (Chicago: University of Chicago Press, 1960). Guthrie's *The Greeks and Their Gods* (London: Methuen, 1968) compares the Olympian gods, whom man cannot touch, and the dark gods of the underground (and the unconscious), who promise life in death to mortals. See also Morse Peckham, *Beyond the Tragic Vision: The Quest for Identity in the Nineteenth Century* (New York: George Braziller, 1962), for a study of the psychological pattern of "orientation" (Peckham's term) to "disorientation" to new orientation, which marked the work of such authors as Carlyle, Balzac, Wagner, and Nietzsche. Peckham says that preenlightenment orientations gave way in close correlation with increasing religious doubt and individualism. But Blake and other English romantics sought their own way along this path well before Peckham's model, Carlyle, spoke through Professor Teufelsdröckh.

4. Given this density of pain, one might expect the *Songs* to seem gloomy, but few serious readers think of them in such terms. Various factors distance us from the suffering in the poems, apart from our natural tendency to turn away from pain. Most important is that we see each of Blake's distraught characters in a psychological context interesting for its own sake. Other reasons include Blake's strong implicit (sometimes explicit) view that life's pleasures may balance or even outweigh its pains, and that it is at least possible that we may be saved; certainly all of his energy for living is directed by the artist-prophet's expectations of Eternity, in one way or another. Finally, Blake, unlike Wordsworth, for example, does not identify a single voice that might be taken, however mistakenly, as autobiographical, so that any pain it expressed could be understood to be Blake's own. Indeed, he uses such voices—in *Milton,* for instance—but in Blake's world, they are surrounded by "other" voices not "his own." Pain is distributed, not heaped on a single tragic vehicle in his world.

5. Northrop Frye, *Fearful Symmetry* (Princeton, N.J.: Princeton University Press, 1947), says about the origins of Selfhood, "We are born into a fallen world and are therefore born with a 'natural' tendency to make the most rather than the best of it, to accept it as final reality. . . . But the polities of the wolf pack and the beehive are not good enough for us. Both the tyrant and his victim are in a state of nature, and both are in that state of animal self-absorption which Blake calls the Selfhood" (p. 58). This suggests to me that the selfish tendency which wants "to make the most" of the world has some basis in a blind unthinking will to be—a kind of "natural" primary counterforce to nonbeing. A close parallel is La Rochefoucauld's "Self-love," defined in the first of the "Maximes Supprimées." There he refers to it less as a self-serving agent of mind than as a tenacious being, without primary attributes

except tenacity. "The obscurity that conceals [Self-love]... never keeps it from seeing clearly... [the dangers to itself] beyond its own limits.... It thrives everywhere, in all circumstances, living off everything, off nothing; it accommodates itself to all things and to their absence.... In short, it wants to exist, and so long as it does, it is [even] willing to be its own enemy." *La Rochefoucauld Maximes,* ed. Jacques Truchet (Paris: Garnier Frères, 1967), pp. 133–36. My translation.

6. Robert F. Gleckner, *The Piper and the Bard* (Detroit: Wayne State University Press, 1959), cautions against a usual reading of the poem "as a social document" (p. 108), though he does so for different reasons from mine. Incidentally, the predicament of chimney sweepers in Blake's day, important for an understanding of certain levels of the poem, is well identified by Martin K. Nurmi, "Fact and Symbol in 'The Chimney Sweeper'... ," in *Blake: A Collection of Critical Essays,* ed. Northrop Frye (Englewood Cliffs, N.J.: Prentice-Hall, 1966), pp. 15–22.

7. Joseph H. Wicksteed, *Blake's Innocence and Experience* (London: J. M. Dent & Sons 1928), credits John Sampson with implying the word's two meanings by placing an apostrophe "before the four times repeated 'weep' to suggest that the little boy's cry [also] meant 'sweep.' " See Sampson's edition, *The Poetical Works of William Blake* (Oxford: Clarendon Press, 1905), p. 97.

8. Gleckner believes the speaker "is in reality the instigator of [the dream], or perhaps the inspiration" (p. 110). Harold Bloom, *Blake's Apocalypse* (Garden City, N.Y.: Doubleday, 1963), implies the dream belongs to both boys when he refers to "their own liberating dream" (p. 40). Zachary Leader, *Reading Blake's "Songs"* (London: Routledge & Kegan Paul, 1981), like Wicksteed and Gleckner, sees a connection between the words of comfort and the dream: "The very existence of the dream seems to owe something to the older sweep's influence" (p. 45). None of these commentators explores the suggestion by taking it to the text to see how it might work there as the basis of an extended comment.

9. An interesting congruence and differentiation may be observed in Hobbes and Blake on death as a conditioning force. Like Blake, Hobbes believed that we cannot avoid confronting the dangers around us, and that the confrontation intimidates and redefines us by reason of our "continual fear... of violent death." Like Blake again, Hobbes believed that death also triumphs if one tries to avoid danger: "to forsake the course is to die" (*The English Works of Thomas Hobbes,* 11 vols., ed. Sir William Molesworth [London: John Bohn, 1829–45], 4:53). And just as Blake's Innocence of pleasure may be said to precede his Experience of dread, so Hobbes understands the quest of fulfillment to come before the fear of death, which eventually governs all our lives. Thomas Spragens, *The Politics of Motion* (Lexington, Ky.: University Press of Kentucky, 1973), explains that for Hobbes, "life is logically prior to joy, but the quest for joy antedates the quest for self-preservation" (p. 195). But then Blake and Hobbes part company. Hobbes regards these accommodations (formations of Selfhood) as "rational" (*Works of Hobbes,* 2: vii) and naturally acceptable for the sake of the Commonwealth. Blake, of course, regards them as part of a process that finally requires their undoing.

10. *Blake's Composite Art* (Princeton, N.J.: Princeton University Press, 1978), pp. 95–96.

11. Mitchell, p. 96.

12. David V. Erdman, *The Illuminated Blake* (Garden City, N.Y.: Anchor Press/ Doubleday, 1974), p. 53, points out that if the figure had been an angel, it would have had wings.

13. Bloom, p. 47.

14. Mitchell, p. 78. Despite the date on the title page (1789), Plate 6 and "Thel's Motto" were not etched before 1791. (See David V. Erdman, ed. *The Complete Poetry and Prose of William Blake,* rev. ed. [Berkeley and Los Angeles: University of California Press, 1982], p. 790.) In some important sense, then, Blake was at work on *The Book of Thel* between the time *Songs of Innocence* and the time *Songs of Experience* appeared.

15. Diana Hume George, *Blake and Freud* (Ithaca, N.Y.: Cornell University Press, 1980), seems to make the same point when she observes that " 'the return of the repressed' for Thel is not a slow process resulting in symptom formation, but rather an instant, naked confrontation" (p. 94). George goes on to appropriate as correct Freud's late-developed view (which she says Blake anticipates) that "fear of mortality is ultimately revealed [in *The Book of Thel*] as a cover for fear of sexuality" (p. 95). Though I agree with her that for Blake sexuality exerts "pressure toward death as well as life" (p. 95), I do not see that Thel's fear of death is a cover for her fear of sex. It seems to me that for Thel death and sexuality include each other; one might say she is without the cumulative experience that would have made the differentiation possible. Brenda S. Webster, *Blake's Prophetic Psychology* (Athens, Ga.: The University of Georgia Press, 1983), sees Blake's poetry, *The Book of Thel* included, as being primarily a means of access into the poet's interior life or psychic "nature." Accordingly she understands Thel to be an invention by means of which Blake both manages sexuality and reveals (unconsciously) the shapes of his own libidinal needs; theoretically, then, Thel is not available as a being or character independent of her author. Webster nevertheless treats sexuality and death in Thel's (in some sense Blake's) imagination, making neither dominant over the other, making both subordinate to the fear of being devoured. Referring to the lines "And all shall say, without a use this shining woman liv'd, / Or did she only live. to be at death the food of worms," Webster observes, "The worm's sexual connotations have long since been noted by critics who see it as symbolic of the sexuality Thel fears. The reaction of most of these readers to Thel's reluctance is to preach at her—as the Cloud does—and insist that she ought to give herself freely. These readers do not seem to appreciate that the prospect of being eaten by worms—death [and sex] as a devouring—might be terrifying to anyone" (p. 52).

16. Mitchell, p. 106.

17. Mitchell, pp. 82–83.

18. Mitchell, pp. 96–99. Similarly, Christopher Heppner, " 'A Desire of Being': Identity and *The Book of Thel,*" *Colby Library Quarterly,* 13, 2 (June 1977), says Thel cannot "see her external world as part of herself" (p. 85), because her self-consciousness gets in the way. He further says, arguing from definitions of "identity" available to Blake in Locke, Hume, and Swedenborg, that Thel lacks identity's "multi-dimensional structure," which he associates with visionary capacity, elements of which are beyond our conscious control (p. 85). But he takes the matter no further psychologically or with reference to Selfhood. Anne Kostelanetz Mellor,

Blake's Human Form Divine (Berkeley, University of California Press, 1974), undercuts my argument concerning Thel's special Selfhood by claiming that metaphorically Thel grows "in the poem from a child to a woman" (p. 21), learning the lesson that her fear of the natural world is misguided, and "that in the world of Innocence, everything is loved and cherished and everything has a unique and worthwhile function" (p. 27). On the other hand, Mellor understands Plate 6, added late, to represent a point of view Blake developed after completing Plate 5: "Blake tried to interpolate into *Thel* his growing conviction that Innocence must both preserve its own integrity and also pit itself against the evils of tyrannical lawgivers" (p. 32). It is on this basis that Mellor finds Thel's return to Har as a "deliberate rejection of the self-imprisoned, sterile, and destructive way of life found in the 'land of death' " (p. 38).

19. Erdman, *Blake's Complete Poetry and Prose,* pp. 487, 733.

20. S. Foster Damon, *William Blake: His Philosophy and Symbols* (Gloucester, Mass.: Peter Smith, 1958; first published by Houghton Mifflin, 1924), p. 282, is in the vanguard of those who offer this interpretation. Wicksteed, p. 253, sees it the same way, and so does Bloom, p. 137.

21. David V. Erdman, *The Notebook of William Blake* (Oxford: Clarendon Press, 1973), p. 109 reversed, contains the Ms. draft.

22. Erdman, *The Illuminated Blake,* p. 85.

23. Erdman, *Blake's Complete Poetry and Prose,* p. 260.

Chapter 3

1. In one of his references to the ordering principle of the creation itself (for Blake "an act of Mercy"), Frye puts it this way: "This world is pervaded by a force we call natural law, and natural law, however mindless and automatic, at any rate affords a solid bottom to life: it provides a sense for the predictable and trustworthy on which the imagination may build." See "Blake's Introduction to Experience," in *Blake: A Collection of Critical Essays,* ed. Northrop Frye (Englewood Cliffs, N.J.: Prentice-Hall, 1966), p. 28.

2. Harold Bloom, *Blake's Apocalypse* (Garden City, N.Y.: Doubleday, 1963), p. 130. In *The Four Zoas,* Blake explains that "The Eternal Man . . . sat down upon the Couches of Beulah / Sorrowful that he could not put off his new risen body / In mental flames the flames refusd they drove him back to Beulah / His body was redeemd to be permanent thro the Mercy Divine" (125:36–39).

3. David V. Erdman, *The Illuminated Blake* (Garden City, N.Y.: Anchor Press/ Doubleday, 1974), says, "I incline to interpret this figure as the bard, aloft in clouds on a prophetic scroll from which he can see 'Present, Past, & Future' . . . or the human form of The Holy Word, which would account for the halo. . . . Both Keynes and Grant hold that this reclining figure must be Earth herself, who is shown in somewhat this posture arising at the lark's call in *L'Allegro* 2 and at the nativity of Jesus in the watercolor for Milton's Nativity Hymn. . . . But Earth in these scenes lies

very much on the earth or on the grass." (p. 72). D. G. Gillham, *William Blake* (Cambridge: Cambridge University Press, 1973), pp. 49–50.

4. Erdman, *The Illuminated Blake,* p. 72.

5. W. J. T. Mitchell, *Blake's Composite Art* (Princeton, N.J.: Princeton University Press, 1978), may be making the same or a similar point when he says "The 'Introduction' to *Experience* presents the 'Voice of the Bard' who . . . transmits the 'Holy Word / . . . Calling the lapsed Soul. . . .' What Earth hears, however, is not the Bard calling her to rise up, but the 'Selfish father of men who accuses and punishes' " (p. 90n). Even if Mitchell intends to imply only that Earth is in no state to hear the Bard *qua* Bard, his comment may be taken to support the idea of an Earth-internalized "Selfish father of men."

6. Bloom says, "the Bard . . . thinks of man as a 'lapsed Soul,' and Blake of course does not. . . . The Bard's dualism, traditional in orthodox Christian accounts of apocalypse, divides still further an already dangerous division" (pp. 130–31). Frye also pauses over "lapsed Soul," but he decides against taking it in its orthodox Christian meaning because the rest of the poem makes it clear that "the conquest of nature is now within man's powers, and is a conquest to which the poets and prophets are summoning him with the voice of the Word of God" (p. 26). A look at the *OED* shows that "soul" is often enough used to mean "person" rather than "disembodied spirit." And "*lapsare,*" from which "lapse" derives, means "to slip" or "to stumble," as well as "to fall." The etymological fact by itself might not mean very much, except that Blake's "other" Bard of the *Songs,* whom we know through "The Voice of the Ancient Bard," identifies humans who are "fallen" and "who stumble all night over bones of the dead" in a context that promises earthly redemption.

7. *The Marriage of Heaven and Hell,* 4.

8. Though for Blake the world could be seen as terrifying (his Thel sees it that way), I shall continue to argue that he believed it is within the power of the imagination, through the psychological examination of one's Selfhood, to control the sense of death that is the root cause of terror. I can understand the reasons for concluding with E. D. Hirsch, *Innocence and Experience* (New Haven, Conn.: Yale University Press, 1964), that "To Tirzah" marks "a return to Blake's primordial faith in the Atonement, in the saving agencies of Mercy, Pity, Peace, and Love" (p. 147). But I do not weigh the evidence as he does. The apparent "pessimism" and "optimism" of the *Songs of Innocence and of Experience* are well explained by Blake's very unusual capacity to see the world at its most frightening, without being so much frightened as moved to see beyond the threats to a higher integration of things. They are much less well explained by his "naturalism" than Hirsch claims they are (pp. 58–87). Blake was always a social reformer, but he did not believe social reform could provide the ultimate amelioration.

9. Hirsch, pp. 106–8.

10. David V. Erdman, *Blake: Prophet Against Empire* (Princeton, N.J.: Princeton University Press, 1954), reminds us that Oliver Elton called "London" Blake's "mightiest brief poem," to which Erdman adds that the poem is "infinite curses in a little room, a world at war in a grain of London soot" (p. 255), implying to one who recalls "a World in a Grain of Sand" that the poem is an "eternity" of a very negative

sort indeed. Bloom says, "The Human Abstract" is the "terrible image of the Tree of Mystery, growing out of the human brain and darkening vision with thickest shades" (p. 142). About both of these poems, Hazard Adams, *William Blake* (Seattle: University of Washington Press, 1963), either states or implies that the capacity to see to the center of satanic things is to reach the point from which "one again turns upward" (p. 285).

11. The poem as a whole supports the view that the speaker is in a heightened state of observation, probably moving along an unpremeditated course, seeing things he may have seen before without apprehending them as he does during the time of his present wandering. The fact that, by wandering, he finds such a totality of destructive and destroyed things, and nothing saving or saved, implies the absence of all else in London. The word "wander" itself reinforces the idea of the speaker's lack of premeditation and the idea that he is outside his customary world of vision and perhaps outside his customary world of peace too. The *OED* includes these meanings for "wander": "To move hither and thither without fixed course or aim"; "To have no fixed abode or station"; "To go or take one's way casually or without predetermined route"; "To deviate from a given path or determined course"; "to stray from one's home or company, or from protection or control." Michael Ferber, "'London' and Its Politics," *ELH*, 48, 2 (1981), 310–38, discusses some of the ways in which critics of the poem have understood "wander" (pp. 313–15). He concludes this section of his essay by referring "London" to *Jerusalem*: "When Blake returned to the motif of a walker through London streets some ten years later (*Jerusalem*, plates 45 and 82 to 85), the walker is Los, who by this time in *Jerusalem* has begun the work of redemption, and [is] not an errant soul with limited vision. He does not wander lost; he is the watchman who searches the interiors of Albion to find out why everyone is degraded or murdered" (pp. 314–15). Though I agree with Ferber's view that "it is too simple to claim [as Adams does, p. 280] that 'Los and Blake and the speaker of "London" are the same'" (p. 344n), I think one ought to remain open to the idea that the wanderer's new view of things in "London" is promising for his redemption, a conclusion which Ferber, in his excellent article, acknowledges to be an important part of Adams's view (p. 332).

12. *OED*. An additional weight may be given to "mark" here, from a use outside the poem. Recall the Bard's song, in *Milton*, where a similar marking of the signs of woe is identified as necessary for redemption: "Mark well my words! they are of your eternal salvation."

13. Ferber identifies the cycle in a slightly different way: "After the general *every Man* there is a sequence of youthful victims, perhaps in order of age (infant, sweeper, soldier, harlot), and then the last of them victimizes the first and starts the cycle over again" (p. 312).

14. For a clear argument about the "blood down Palace walls" as an omen of mutiny and regicide, see Erdman, *Prophet Against Empire*, pp. 256–58.

15. Frye, *Fearful Symmetry* (Princeton, N.J.: Princeton University Press, 1947), for example, sees the natural or fallen world as giving rise to "tyranny as the defense of [that] world and of liberty as the effort of the imagination to recover the

state of innocence" (p. 182), though Orc, an early instrument of the effort at recovery, is modified in various senses by Blake over time. Bloom says, "Of the four stanzas of *London* only the third is really about the oppression of man by society. The other three emphasize man's all-too-natural repression of his own freedom" (p. 140).

16. Frye, "Blake's Introduction to Experience," effectively explains the psychology of fear: "Man makes a gigantic idol out of the dark world [of fallen nature], and is so impressed by its stupidity, cruelty, empty spaces, and automatism that he tries to live in accordance with the dreary ideals it suggests. He naturally assumes that his god is jealous of everything he clings to with secret longing and wants it surrendered to him; hence he develops a religion of sacrifice" (p. 30).

17. Erdman, *Prophet Against Empire,* in the chapter "O Voltaire! Rousseau!" (pp. 387–93), makes a persuasive case for Blake's ambivalence, divided as he seems to be between revolution and patient forgiveness: "Blake's political ambivalence stands out sharply in his notebook jottings and marginalia of 1808–1812. 'If Men were Wise, the Most arbitrary Princes could not hurt them,' and Blake is 'really sorry to see my countrymen trouble themselves about Politics.' Yet he cannot refrain from exclaiming the Princes and their Hirelings have hurt *him* deeply, nor from crying with Solomon: 'Oppression makes the Wise Man Mad' " (pp. 391–92). Erdman also remarks Blake's pleasure in the passage of the Slave Trade Bill in 1807 and in action taken against the corruption surrounding the sale of army commissions (p. 392). Redemption, not politics, must provide the final solution of the problems of a failing society, but political reform is inseparable from the redemption of men and women in society.

18. Blake shared the growing belief in the age that men and women could free themselves from the tyrannies of false education and entrenched authority and control their own fates to build a new Jerusalem. The difference between him and others may be measured best by his sense for the difficulties to be overcome. The speakers of "London" and "The Human Abstract" (see below) and Thel at her "own grave plot" imply those difficulties, as does Blake's sense for the mind's complexity in Self-deception generally and the closely related tenacity of Selfhood. His fellow romantics in different ways came to conclusions about the mind very like Blake's. Among his other contemporaries there was a range of optimism, sometimes pretty facile. For example, though not a simple idealist by any means, Godwin believed man's mind and worldly condition could be enormously improved. (Note the word "Happiness" in the full title of *Political Justice,* below.) He held the mind was formed by conditioning—accidental, preceptoral, and social conditioning, for which last "the forms of government under which we live" are responsible. Almost always temperately expressed, his views could be radically optimistic, as, for example, this one: "Multitudes . . . [might] exert the energy necessary to extraordinary success . . . [if] they [would] dismiss the prejudices that fetter them, get rid of the chilling system of occult and inexplicable causes, and consider the human mind as an intelligent agent, guided by motives and prospects presented to the understanding, and not by causes of which we have no proper cognisance. . . . We have been ignorant, we have been hasty, or we have been misled. Remove the causes of this

ignorance or this miscalculation, and the effects will cease" (*Enquiry Concerning Political Justice and Its Influence on Morals and Happiness,* 3 vols., ed. F. E. L. Priestley [Toronto: The University of Toronto Press, 1946], 1:44–45).

The history of social betterment in England, starting in the seventeenth century, includes the establishment of numerous institutions intended to save or improve lives. Many of them were doubtless founded out of a growing sense of social responsibility, supported by a growing technology in medicine, agriculture, manufacture, and distribution. But considered in the context of Blake's poetry, these charitable activities seem pathetic, given their clear inadequacy to solve the social problems of "London" and the more fundamental psychological problem of the mind-forged manacles that perpetuate the chartered city. What they do in fact is indirectly to support the status quo, or help benefactors quite inappropriately to feel the virtue of their charity, as Blake tells us in "The Human Abstract."

19. Though there may be promise in "a beam of strong light" towards which a "vagabond boy" guides "a long-bearded barefoot man with crutches along a cobblestone pavement, past a closed door" (Erdman, *The Illuminated Blake,* p. 88), the man, probably London (*Jerusalem,* 84), is clearly in bad shape. Referring to him as a "crippled old man," and identifying him with Urizen, Hirsch says, "the weakness and woe he symbolizes is also the weakness and woe he has caused" (p. 265). The illustration to "London" also includes a naked child warming himself at an outdoor fire. But it is mind's, not body's, plight one sees in the illustration to "The Human Abstract," where an old man, probably "Cruelty," is being snared in a net that seems to emanate from his own head.

20. As I have earlier indicated, Adams very much sees it this way: " 'London,' through the fierce delineation of its vision, becomes an affirmative poem.... For Blake, to see error in its completed form is to vitiate its power" (p. 285).

21. *Four Zoas,* 117: 5–6. Blake in any age might have had the poetic insight that fear of nonexistence is at the heart of Selfhood's will to stay with the natural world rather than to surrender itself to Self-annihilation and eternity. But in fact men and women of his own age were in special need of the lesson, and probably he too needed its reinforcement from time to time.

22. *Four Zoas,* 109: 32–34.

23. The physical constraints suggest that nature has implied a danger in sexuality by these anatomical means. How then can the imagination avoid the fear built into the body itself might be the question. Thel's reponse is that it cannot. Diana Hume George, *Blake and Freud* (Ithaca, N.Y.: Cornell University Press, 1980), represents Thel's response in Freudian terms, which provide one way of understanding the bond between body and mind at issue here: "The final and decisive boundary for Thel is the hymen, the 'little curtain of flesh.' ... Its invasion by the youthful burning boy on the bed of their mutual desire signifies complete loss of self to Thel, the dissolution of ego boundaries that is experienced in love. That 'boundarilessness' is the very essence of eroticism ... , 'assenting to life to the point of death.' Thel is unable to face [it]" (p. 97).

24. *Milton,* 38:38–41.

25. *Nineteenth-Century Accounts of William Blake,* ed. Joseph Anthony Wittreich, Jr. (Gainesville, Fla.: Scholars' Facsimiles & Reprints, 1970), p. 72.

Chapter 4

1. *Milton,* 32:23. Also see *A Vision of the Last Judgment* [PAGE 79]. Blake also says, "Man Passes on but States remain for Ever he passes thro them like a traveller" (*A Vision,* [PAGE 80]). But as Susan Fox, *Poetic Form in Blake's 'Milton' "* (Princeton, N.J.: Princeton University Press, 1976), points out, "It may be that by 'States Change' Blake meant only that they seem to change for the individuals who pass through them" (p. 23).

2. *Milton,* 35:42, 44.

3. *The Notebook of William Blake,* ed. David V. Erdman (Oxford: Clarendon Press, 1973), pp. 103, 105.

4. Here I have simply made use of the view that "Tirzah . . . stands for man's bondage to nature" (Harold Bloom, *Blake's Apocalypse* [Garden City, N.Y.: Doubleday, 1963], p. 144) and of the biblical text on which Blake draws for the line "The Sexes rose to work & weep": "Unto the woman he said, I will greatly multiply thy sorrow and thy conception; in sorrow thou shalt bring forth children . . . And unto Adam he said . . . , In the sweat of thy face shalt thou eat bread, till thou return unto the ground" (Genesis 3:16, 17, 19). I consider the matter more fully in chapter 6.

5. *Milton,* 3:6.

6. In offering this widely observed conclusion here, I anticipate my argument. One very recent comment on the subject connects Blake's movement of humanity beyond sexual being with his movement through states. "The permanence of states serves their function of freeing individuals. States are permanent so that they may be forever separable from individuals and may forever be thrown off . . . ; sexual identity as male and female is not identity but a state" (Leonard W. Deen, *Conversing in Paradise* [Columbia, Mo.: University of Missouri Press, 1983], p. 214). Susan Fox sensitively comprehends the movement towards unity of being by identifying various aspects of Jesus, the Divine Humanity, as integral with Milton, Ololon, Los (and the Blake character), as they descend, in *Blake's "Milton,"* pp. 92–96.

7. Northrop Frye, "Blake's Introduction to Experience," in *Blake: A Collection of Critical Essays,* ed. Frye (Englewood Cliffs, N.J.: Prentice-Hall, 1966), pp. 23–31, assumes this integration as a well-identified poetic-religious ideal in the first two *Songs of Experience.*

8. *Milton,* 21:15. This sweet River, Ololon, Milton's variable ("parallel") emanation, may be found both in "her Ulro-form of the perverse Rahab/Tirzah, [and] in the full beauty of her eternal portion" (Fox, p. 91).

9. Irene H. Chayes, "Little Girls Lost: Problems of a Romantic Archetype," in *Blake: A Collection of Critical Essays,* ed. Frye, identifies some of the rich dimensions of this burden in terms deriving from her archetypal treatment of Lyca: "She is not only a new adumbration of Persephone, the lost daughter and queen of the Underworld. She is also the sleeping maiden of nursery folklore; an Orphan Child who voluntarily separates herself from her parents; Una, the Christian Kore, a Magdalen who recovers innocence; a second Eve who reverses the Fall; a Dantesque pilgrim who does not flee from the beasts of prey, and perhaps even becomes one of them; Isaiah's 'little child' as redeemer, leading the way for others to follow; a foreshadowing of Blake's own persecuted and exiled Jerusalem, who

prepares to become the bride of the Lamb by first becoming the bride of the lion" (p. 73).

Robert Gleckner, *The Piper and The Bard* (Detroit: Wayne State University Press, 1959), using quite different terms, moved by "hints of sexuality," impresses us with Lyca's emotional burden: "Lyca of her own free will has entered experience or, at least, the half-light before complete darkness; and in this light her abduction by the beasts is perfectly right. They are playful only in the context of prophecy and vision; in reality, experience, they are still beasts of prey after all" (p. 222). Hazard Adams, *William Blake: A Reading of the Shorter Poems* (Seattle: University of Washington Press, 1963), pp. 210–17, also finds Lyca's predicament upsetting to her because her parents "regard her growth as inevitably and ultimately tragic" (p. 211).

10. I follow David V. Erdman's text here—"Witless woe, was ne'er beguiled," *The Complete Poetry and Prose of William Blake,* rev. ed. (Berkeley and Los Angeles: University of California Press, 1982), p. 24. With the comma after "woe," the line raises questions different from those that have occurred to readers who have understood it to have no comma. E. D. Hirsch, Jr., *Innocence and Experience: An Introduction to Blake* (New Haven, Conn.: Yale University Press, 1964), for example, believes "Witless woe was ne'er beguiled" is the speaker's expression of faith in her safety—"a boundless faith in the sanctity of childlike ignorance" (p. 242); Hirsch explains some of the complications in the poem by concluding that Angel "is repelled by her weeping ('So he took his wings and fled') because it is based on the cunning idea that witless woe is never beguiled" (p. 242). D. G. Gillham, *Blake's Contrary States* (Cambridge: Cambridge University Press, 1966), though his assignment of motives is different from mine, comes close to my view in saying that the speaker's manipulated aging leaves her sad and that "the fears she assumes in order to play the coquette are translated into real fears" (p. 137).

11. David V. Erdman, *The Illuminated Blake* (Garden City, N.Y.: Anchor Press/Doubleday, 1974), p. 83.

12. Zachary Leader, *Reading Blake's Songs*" (London: Routledge & Kegan Paul, 1981), says, "The 'virgin queen' of "The Angel" . . . seems lost in moony, miserable self-absorption" (p. 154).

13. *The Illuminated Blake,* p. 183.

14. *Jerusalem,* 59:7–9. Blake indeed shows the way to redemption (as well as the nature of our fallen state) in the *Songs.* Both fall and redemption are very like those that may be inferred from the major prophecies, say, *Jerusalem.* A forecast here may be in order. In his chapter "Renovation," Thomas R. Frosch, *The Awakening of Albion* (Ithaca, N.Y.: Cornell University Press, 1974), discusses all the senses body may use to renew life, but he gives a special place to sexuality. When sexuality is distorted, "the emotional [faculty] becomes a jealous and aggressive natural heart. . . . What we take to be [loving] contact is really a devouring. . . . Further, when the self withdraws from its own substance, the body's capacity for action is diminished . . . ; we lose the connection between desire and act . . . ; refused, the body becomes an instrument, then a cavern . . . ; the liberty of the senses to discover and achieve their own fulfillment is replaced by a self-induced suppression and a feeling of powerlessness" (pp. 134–35). In the following chapter, "The Body of Imagination," Frosch argues persuasively that the atrophied senses, including

touch, may be renovated by Imagination, which is "our whole power, the total functioning interplay of our capacities . . . , a mode of knowing that participates simultaneously in body and soul, a mental work of the senses and feelings" (p. 155). In chapters 5 and 6 below, I explore this "mode of knowing" in the *Songs*.

15. Adams, p. 253.

16. This pattern, apart from the exception I have noted, is broken only once, in the eighth line of "Nurse's Song" (Innocence), and then the rhythm is maintained— "Till the morning appears in the skies."

17. Adams refers to "the strange exaggeration of 'my face turns green and pale' " (p. 253). G. K. Chesterton, *William Blake* (London: Duckworth, n.d.), censures the "monstrous line," saying thereafter that Blake "would mention with as easy an emphasis that a woman's face turned green as that the fields were green when she looked at them" (p. 10). On the other hand, W. Somerset Maugham, *Of Human Bondage* (New York: Garden City Publishing, 1939; first published by William Heinemann, 1915), has no trouble with green and pale skin: "The greenish pallor of [Mildred's] skin intoxicated [Philip], and her thin white lips had an extraordinary fascination" (p. 324), though whether Maugham's imagination here owes something to Blake, I do not know.

18. D. G. Gillham, *William Blake* (Cambridge: Cambridge University Press, 1973), p. 38.

19. Leader says, "The outstretched arm and poised comb, with sharp-pointed teeth . . . , suggest threat and restriction" (p. 154).

20. Adams makes a useful comparison in saying the speaker's relationship to the Sick Rose "recalls the effort of the Bard of 'Introduction' to *Songs of Experience* to bring the sleeping earth to consciousness" (p. 14).

21. Adams, p. 14; Bloom, p. 135; Gillham, *Blake,* pp. 11–12.

22. Bloom, p. 135; Gillham, *Blake,* p. 11; Gleckner, p. 262.

23. Such separateness is assumed, for example, by Bloom: "The worm is borne to the hidden rose bed . . . by the agency of nature ('the howling storm') and his phallic passion devours the rose's life" (p. 135).

24. Adams, p. 209; Bloom, p. 135; Gillham, *Blake's Contrary States,* p. 165.

25. Gleckner says, "Both jealousy and death are involved, and both are united in the image of the worm; the bed on which the secret joys are performed differs little from the grave Thel refused to remain in" (pp. 262–63).

26. C. M. Bowra, *The Romantic Imagination* (London: Oxford University Press, 1961; first published by Harvard University Press, 1950), says with a sure economy, "The flower which turns its head to follow the sun's course and is yet rooted in the earth is Blake's symbol for all men and women whose lives are dominated and spoiled by longing which they can never hope to satisfy, and who are held down to the earth despite their desire for release into some brighter, freer sphere" (p. 45). Just as Adams (p. 14) referred "The Sick Rose" to the Bard's "Introduction" and "Earth's Answer" (see note 20 above), so Leader refers "Ah! Sun-Flower" to the central issue in these first two *Songs of Experience:* "[the poem] represents a sympathetic response to Earth's cry for sexual liberation" (p. 167).

27. Erdman, *The Illuminated Blake,* p. 85.

28. This view assumes that to some extent Blake considers the problem he treats

in his poems from the perspective of his own sex. That he often does so seems beyond doubt. But he does so not because of any artistic incapacity to do otherwise, but because his art is also his religion, and he sometimes adopts a perspective appropriate to his own salvation. As he works along the lines of that salvation, he moves inevitably from the fallen world and towards eternity, and the categories of conventional sexuality are lost in ungendered categories of being, though not before Blake has examined and indicted the destructive modes of both sexes in the fallen world. Blake does not explicitly clarify his sexual usage in the *Songs*. No Ololon and no Milton finally unite in Jesus, having cast off their sexual garments. But we may see his direction if we understand from "Introduction," "Earth's Answer," and other songs that his aim is only incidentally a psychology of the sexes. His ultimate concern is humanity.

29. Diana Hume George, *Blake and Freud* (Ithaca, N.Y.: Cornell University Press, 1980), p. 179.

Chapter 5

1. *A Descriptive Catalogue, The Complete Poetry and Prose of William Blake,* rev. ed., ed. David V. Erdman (Berkeley and Los Angeles: University of California Press, 1982), p. 544.

2. *A Vision of the Last Judgment,* [PAGE 68].

3. *Milton,* 35:42–45.

4. John E. Grant, "Interpreting Blake's 'The Fly,' " in *Blake: A Collection of Critical Essays,* ed. Northrop Frye (Englewood Cliffs, N.J.: Prentice-Hall, 1966), finds difficulties of logic in the last two stanzas: " 'If I live' is a puzzle that [the speaker] himself could not finally explain" (p. 42). Jean H. Hagstrum, "The Fly," in *William Blake: Essays for S. Foster Damon,* ed. Alvin H. Rosenfeld (Providence, R.I.: Brown University Press, 1969), says, "Those lines, which comprise the last stanza, have proved baffling" (p. 380). Hagstrum goes on to suggest that "the last luminous word of the poem is 'happy.' The final two lines come as a denouement. 'If I live or if I die' means simply, 'Whatever befalls me' " (p. 381). Zachary Leader, *Reading Blake's "Songs"* (London: Routledge & Kegan Paul, 1981), includes "The Fly," along with "The Little Vagabond," "The Schoolboy," and "The Garden of Love," among the songs that "leave us vaguely suspicious of their speakers; . . . our sympathy for them takes second place to a sense that we are being misled" (p. 171).

5. Grant, in the Appendix to "Interpreting Blake's 'The Fly,' " argues plausibly that although "the word 'fly' was a generic term meaning 'winged insect' in the eighteenth century . . . , the fly in the poem should be imagined as a housefly" (*Critical Essays,* ed. Frye, p. 52).

6. In making this point, I wish to separate myself from the view that the speaker's vision abrogates "the pragmatic distinction between life and death . . . , [which is to] dehumanize oneself," as Harold Bloom claims (*Blake's Apocalypse* [Garden City, N.Y.: Doubleday, 1963], pp. 136–37). I believe the speaker has a vision

of his own mortality that in fact liberates him from the fallen world much more than it delivers him to it, as Bloom suggests.

7. Though I have no trouble in accepting the line "And strength & breath" as an intensification of the line that precedes it, Grant believes that this "second line . . . is ambiguous. If the speaker is simply saying that 'strength and breath' are attributes of 'life,' he is making an assertion that seems self-evident and even redundant" (*Critical Essays,* ed. Frye, p. 41). But in fact the association of "life" with "breath," "soul," "heart," "mind," and "strength" is to be found in certain biblical parallel constructions. "And the Lord God formed man . . . , and breathed into his nostrils the breath of life; and man became a living soul." (Genesis 2:7); "And [Jesus said] thou shalt love the Lord thy God with all thy heart, and with all thy soul, and with all thy mind, and with all thy strength; this is the first commandment" (Mark 12:30). Redundancy need not be supererogation.

8. Grant, *Critical Essays,* ed. Frye, p. 48. David V. Erdman, *The Illuminated Blake* (Garden City, N.Y.: Anchor Press/Doubleday, 1974), p. 82.

9. Grant, *Critical Essays,* ed. Frye, p. 48n. Erdman, *The Illuminated Blake,* uses almost the same words: "At the last words a bird or bat or moth . . . rises" (p. 82). Later, Grant, who has doubts about the clarity of the poem, but relatively few about the clarity of the picture, narrows down the options further: "The fundamental question . . . is whether the creature depicted . . . has optimistic implications (butterfly) or very optimistic ones (bird). Since the total meaning of the design remains the same in any case, there need to be no confusion if the creature is somewhat arbitrarily called a bird" (p. 55).

10. Grant, *Critical Essays,* ed. Frye, p. 50.

11. Ibid.

12. *A Vision of the Last Judgment,* [PAGE 94].

13. Anne Kostelanetz Mellor, *Blake's Human Form Divine* (Berkeley: University of California Press, 1974), provides a strong endorsement, however oblique, of the view that the speaker of "The Fly" has experienced a redemptive moment: "Both the [Innocent's] instinctive, 'thoughtless' trust in the love and care of God (as in 'The Fly' where the [Innocent] is 'happy' whether he lives or dies) and the consciousness of oneself as the human form divine . . . are equally valid ways of participating in the one true divine vision" (p. 334).

14. Grant, "The Art and Argument of 'The Tyger,'" in *Discussions of William Blake,* ed. Grant (Boston: D. C. Heath, 1961), p. 64.

15. Grant, *Discussions of Blake,* p. 65. Though unlike Grant, Morton D. Paley, "Tyger of Wrath," *PMLA,* 81, 7 (December 1966), does not concern himself with the character or the psychology of the speaker, he offers a brilliant reading of the poem, which he understands to be "an apostrophe to Wrath [the wrath of the Old Testament God] as a 'sublime' phenomenon. . . . In the Old Testament Prophets, divine wrath is often associated with a Day of Yahweh which will accomplish the destruction of evil and establish a community of the righteous" (p. 542). Paley locates the good effects of the apostrophe largely in the world outside the poem's speaker; but he also expresses sympathy for the idea that the speaker himself may be transformed, by quoting from Boehme's *The Threefold Life of Man* in this

connection: " 'Such a soul is *easy* to be awakened . . . especially when the Hammer of the Holy Ghost sounds through the Ears into the Heart, then the tincture of the soul receives it *instantly;* and there it goes forth through the whole soul' " (p. 550).

16. Joseph H. Wicksteed, *Blake's Innocence and Experience* (New York: E. P. Dutton, 1928), p. 198.

17. Grant, *Discussions of Blake,* p. 80.

18. Ibid., p. 75.

19. *For the Sexes,* in Erdman, *Poetry and Prose of William Blake,* p. 260.

20. Wicksteed, p. 198.

21. Martin K. Nurmi, "Blake's Revisions of *The Tyger,*" *PMLA* 71, 4 (September 1956): 672.

22. Grant, *Discussions of Blake,* pp. 73–75.

23. Ibid., p. 79.

24. Erdman, *The Illuminated Blake,* p. 84.

Chapter 6

1. Robert F. Gleckner, *The Piper and The Bard* (Detroit: Wayne State University Press, 1959), for example, says of "A Poison Tree": "The . . . murder [of the speaker's foe] is the prevention of act in another, just as act was prevented in self. That for Blake was the only kind of evil, a negation" (p. 258). Heather Glen, *Vision and Disenchantment: Blake's "Songs" and Wordsworth's "Lyrical Ballads"* (Cambridge: Cambridge University Press, 1983), says of the poem's last stanza that it "is superficially a statement of triumph: the 'foe' is dead and the speaker is 'glad.' Yet after the self-negating, self-abasing and finally self-obliterating process which the poem has traced, this attempt to affirm feeling has a curious hollowness" (p. 192). D. G. Gillham, *Blake's Contrary States* (Cambridge: Cambridge University Press, 1966), says of "To Tirzah": "The preoccupation with the natural body in the poem is unhealthy, the speaker cannot find satisfaction of an 'earthy' sort but hangs on to the idea that he will obtain it. He is at once repelled and fascinated by the flesh and his notion of eternity is of endless time spent in a body that is, somehow, not a body" (p. 235).

2. With Gleckner (see note 1 above), Harold Bloom, *Blake's Apocalypse* (Garden City, N.Y.: Doubleday, 1963), sees the poem as a study of constraint, "a grisly meditation on the natural consequences of repressed anger" (p. 144).

3. Gillham, *William Blake* (Cambridge: Cambridge University Press, 1973), in fact faults the speaker, who "is too exultant to realize how much damage he has done himself, though he is aware that the triumph is basely taken" (p. 136).

4. David V. Erdman, *The Illuminated Blake* (Garden City, N.Y.: Anchor Press/Doubleday, 1974), p. 91. As Erdman points out, it is only in "some copies" that his hand (or my serpent's head) can be found.

5. Before arguing that "To Tirzah" is a palinode—"a sweeping repudiation of all the preceding poems of Experience"—E. D. Hirsch, Jr., *Innocence and Experi-*

ence (New Haven, Conn.: Yale University Press, 1964), explains the ways in which the late-added song is "utterly unlike any of the other *Songs*" (pp. 290, 281–82).

6. Bloom, says, " 'To Tirzah' is a condensed summary of the entire cycle of *Songs of Innocence and of Experience*" (p. 144). Gleckner, pp. 269–71, offers similar comments on "To Tirzah" and so does Hazard Adams, *William Blake* (Seattle: University of Washington Press, 1963), pp. 272–75.

7. Henry Crabb Robinson records that Blake told him "Christ ought not to have suffered himself to be crucified. He should not have attacked the Government. He had no business with such matters." See *Nineteenth-Century Accounts of William Blake,* ed. Joseph Anthony Wittreich, Jr. (Gainesville, Fla.: Scholars' Facsimiles & Reprints, 1970), p. 90. "Everlasting Gospel," PAGES 48–52, 11. 91–92. Leslie Tannenbaum, *Biblical Tradition in Blake's Early Prophecies: The Great Code of Art* (Princeton, N.J.: Princeton University Press, 1982), points out that for Blake, "emblems or types of Christ [occur in] original forms . . . dictated by God and copied by artists of all nations, so that art becomes . . . the organization of human perception and experience . . . according to a divine pattern" (p. 100). But she also observes that we find Blake, in talking about Christ, "sometimes expressing a fairly orthodox point of view and other times giving the doctrine some radical twists" (p. 82).

8. Crabb Robinson, *Nineteenth-Century Accounts,* tells us that in "speaking of the Atonement in the ordinary Calvinistic sense, [Blake] said, 'It is a horrible doctrine; if another pay your debt, I do not forgive it' " (p. 107). Jean H. Hagstrum, "Christ's Body," in *William Blake, Essays in Honour of Sir Geoffrey Keynes,* eds. Morton D. Paley and Michael Phillips (Oxford: Clarendon Press, 1973), pp. 129–56, understands Blake to have held this view in an important, though not dominant, tradition of similar belief, which included Priestley, who "found the doctrine of substitutionary atonement of Christ a 'gross misrepresentation of the character and the moral government of God,' a doctrine 'greatly disfiguring and depraving' the 'scheme of Christianity' " (p. 132). As I have noted before, Hirsch offers an extensively argued contrary view in his discussion of "To Tirzah," claiming the poem marks "a return to Blake's primordial faith in the Atonement, in the saving agencies of Mercy, Pity, Peace, and Love" (p. 147).

9. Hirsch, pp. 106–48. The doubts implicit in the sequence of his revisions of *Vala or the Four Zoas* (c. 1796–1807?) have been explained as a function of this deep concern, and the explanation has been applied to the Tirzah poem. Though Erdman does not address this question in his textual discussion of *The Four Zoas,* he dismisses all claims based on a presumed knowledge of Blake's stages of composition: "The complexities of the [*Four Zoas*] ms, in short, continue to defy analysis and all assertions about meaningful physical groupings or chronologically definable layers of composition or inscription must be understood to rest on partial and ambiguous evidence." *The Complete Poetry and Prose of William Blake,* rev. ed. (Berkeley and Los Angeles: University of California Press, 1982), p. 818.

10. In Numbers 27:1–11, 36:3, and Joshua 17:3–4, is told the story of Tirzah, the fifth of five daughters born to Zelophehad, who fathered no sons. Upon the father's death, they were assigned his inheritance, in the absence of male heirs, with the result (in Blake's world) that they take on the destructive power of Female Will.

11. Hagstrum, *Essays ... Keynes,* comments effectively on the distinction between Blake's feeling of kinship with Christ and his independence of Him—"of Blake's ... portrayal of Christ we may use the term identification but not absorption. ... Union, yes; fusion, no. Christian oneness, yes; mystical, Neoplatonic, Oriental, Gnostic unity, no. From that kind of vagueness ... Blake was preserved by his conception of the body of Christ. A body may be attracted to another body, but it is also the nature of a body to resist absorption and to keep some kind of distance" (p. 154).

12. Erdman, *The Illuminated Blake,* p. 94.

13. Erdman, *The Illuminated Blake,* p. 388, tells us that even in the seven copies of the *Songs* that end with a poem other than "To Tirzah," in which the Tirzah poem is followed only by "The School Boy" and "The Voice of the Ancient Bard," there is a terminal hint of apocalypse. Zachary Leader, *Reading Blake's "Songs"* (London: Routledge & Kegan Paul, 1982), p. 200, stresses that only a few copies of the *Songs* (E, I, O, and S) are concluded with "To Tirzah," and expresses discomfort with what he believes to be a weakness in Erdman's view about apocalypse—that the reader would have to allow for Blake's abrupt introduction of the subject in the *Songs.* But in fact *Songs of Experience* are about apocalypse; that is, they are about individual redemption that presupposes a casting out of nature.

14. Kathleen Raine, *Blake and Tradition,* 2 vols. (Princeton, N.J.: Princeton University Press, 1968), 1: 397n. Raine cites Keynes and supports his view.

15. Erdman, *The Illuminated Blake,* p. 94.

16. "This is the Race that Jesus ran / Humble·to God Haughty to Man / ... that which was of Woman born / In the absence of the Morn / ... Lifes *dim* Windows of the Soul / Distorts the Heavens from Pole to Pole / And leads you to Believe a Lie / When you see with not thro the Eye." *The Notebook of William Blake,* ed. David V. Erdman (Oxford: Clarendon Press, 1973), pp. 53–54.

17. Though I agree with Bloom that "Blake understands the Atonement as the Triumph of the imaginative body over the natural body" (p. 145), his primary claim, that Tirzah has not been able to "bind or close the [speaker's] fifth sense, the specifically sexual sense of touch" (p. 245), and that it is on this sense that his liberation is based, seems misleading. She has constrained her son's sight, smell, hearing, speech, and "feelings"—("the heart Pathos"). What chance would his "free" sense of touch have for gratifying sexuality, unless he were able to "cleanse" his senses by understanding how he has been taken in? His touch would otherwise be barren. Thomas R. Frosch, *The Awakening of Albion* (Ithaca, N.Y.: Cornell University Press, 1974), refers accurately to tactile sense in Blake as "one of the rarest qualities. There is plenty of pawing and laying hold, but no real touch" (p. 133). Morton D. Paley, *The Continuing City: William Blake's "Jerusalem"* (Oxford: Clarendon Press, 1983), has given us a new sense for just how complicated Blake's view of sexuality is, especially in his chapter "The Myth of Humanity"; a fallen imagination has resulted in "the division of androgynous humankind into two sexes, the limitation of direct sensuous experience to one of the fallen Zoas (Tharmas), and the concentration of sexual pleasure in the genital organs" (p. 201). Surely a reversal of this sexual reduction requires imaginative as well as tactile sponsorship.

18. *Jerusalem,* 3.

19. Leopold Damrosch, Jr., *Symbol and Truth in Blake's Myth* (Princeton, N.J.: Princeton University Press, 1980), considers the details of Blake's repudiation in an interesting discussion of will, pp. 134–36.

20. For a useful review of ideas about self that serve as a context in which Blake may be better understood in this regard, see William Dennis Horn, "William Blake and the Problematic of the Self," in *William Blake and the Moderns,* eds. Robert J. Bertholf and Annette S. Levitt (Albany, N.Y.: State University of New York Press, 1982), pp. 260–85. Horn argues not only that Blake's poetry is concerned with "the painful revelation of the temporal self; 'In anguish of regeneration! in terrors of self annihilation' " (p. 282), but also that it is part of "a movement which expresses the painful experience of abandoning our erroneous notion of a nontemporal self" (p. 283). But he does so by implying that the recognition of loss of one's temporal self is somehow identical with the recognition of the nonexistence of a nontemporal self, a conclusion Blake would have resisted, for reasons I shall consider in chapter 7.

21. *Milton,* 40:34–35.

22. *Milton,* 40:36.

23. W. J. T. Mitchell, *Blake's Composite Art* (Princeton, N.J.: Princeton University Press, 1978), identifies this continuity of need for an ordering principle by referring to Self-annihilation as "the central focus in Blake's vision of personal and collective apocalypse, the imaginative act in which an old Selfhood dies and a new one is born" (p. 149).

24. *Milton,* 32:35.

25. Stuart Curran, "The Structures of *Jerusalem,*" in *Blake's Sublime Allegory,* eds. Curran and Joseph Anthony Wittreich, Jr. (Madison, Wisc.: The University of Wisconsin Press, 1973), pp. 329–46, explains that man "must experience his own crucifixion repeatedly until he comprehends that his defenses against death have walled him apart from life, that the logical outcome of his craving for 'a solid without fluctuation' (*U* 4:10) is death" (p. 343).

26. Blake's autograph in the album of William Upcott is to the point, Blake saying of himself there, "Born 28 Novr 1757 in London & has died several times since." See Erdman, *Poetry and Prose of William Blake,* p. 698.

27. *Jerusalem,* 55:64–65. Nelson Hilton, "An Original Story," in *Unnam'd Forms: Blake and Textuality,* eds. Hilton and Thomas A. Vogler (Berkeley: University of California Press, 1986), in speaking of Oothoon's knowledge of vision in *Visions of the Daughters of Albion,* considers the redemptive struggle for identity in the terms of levels of perception: "We see, and we see our not seeing; we know and know that we know only in part. The issue is not 'ambiguity' or logical contradiction but the experience of various levels, or 'folds,' or perception: contradictions in the logic of identity" (p. 101).

28. Even though their repudiations are not complete, the perceptions of all three boys include some recognition of death in the world that constrains them. The first finds the "Church is cold"; the second is clothed "in the clothes of death"; and the third is threatened with being a "nip'd bud."

29. 1 Peter 3:18: "For Christ . . . died for sins once for all . . . that he might bring us to God, being put to death in the flesh but made alive in the spirit."

30. John E. Grant, "The Art and the Argument of *The Tyger*," in *Discussions of William Blake,* ed. Grant (Boston: D. C. Heath, 1961), makes this identification, p. 79.

31. Romans 7:9–11.

32. Various forms of this view may be found in the Old and New Testaments, e.g., Genesis 48:16; Psalms 23, 26, and 49; Romans 3:21–26 and 18:8–23; 1 Corinthians 2:6–7. According to *The Interpreter's Bible,* 4 vols., ed. George Arthur Buttrick (New York: Abingdon Press, 1962), "The concept of God's saving work among men as a process of redemption from possession or control by an alien power is . . . one of the fundamental concepts of the Bible" (4:22).

Chapter 7

1. Throughout my discussion of the relationship between individual and universal mind or individual and divine humanity, I hold to the view I have assumed throughout this book, that though no act of will can effect redemption, each of us is responsible for his or her own salvation. True, there is a logic (an intermittent logic) in Blake's world, which supports the conclusion that the *realized* divine or complete humanity may somehow be of use to individuals who are themselves *struggling to realize* their completeness. Jesus is "available" to us, a given of the universe. But in fact the major thrust of Blake's poetry is not the movement from completeness (or universal or divine) to individual, but from individual to universal. This direction may very well result from the chronology of Blake's own religious experience. It certainly takes into account the human predicament; it is a chronology we all share with him. For more on this subject see chapter 1, note 14, above.

2. Leopold Damrosch, Jr., *Symbol and Truth in Blake's Myth* (Princeton, N.J.: Princeton University Press, 1980), p. 21.

3. William Dennis Horn, "William Blake and the Problematic of the Self," in *William Blake and the Moderns,* eds. Robert J. Bertholf and Annette S. Levitt (Albany, N.Y.: State University of New York Press, 1982), pp. 263–64.

4. *Milton,* 32:23.

5. I see the Ancient Mariner irreconcilably divided between a Blakean redemption and some order of orthodox Christian redemption.

6. Though it is usual to think of the Indian Maid as finally revealed to be Cynthia, a change effected by Cynthia's simply stepping out of her disguise, "an effortless, mechanical transformation" (Barry Gradman, *Metamorphosis in Keats* [New York: New York University Press, 1980], p. 17), it is the case that Keats observes a distinction throughout the poem between Endymion's conscious longings and judgments about himself (many of which prove to be wrong) and the process of his transformation from earthling, about which he is largely unconscious. The Indian Maid/Cynthia episode is only the last in a very long series of experiences illustrating this bifurcation, which it also concludes. The identification of Indian Maid as Cynthia is Endymion's identification, finally, his hard-won vision

that makes earth continuous with the heavens and Endymion himself immortal. I do not mean to say that *Endymion* is a faultless work of art. But any shortcomings it may suffer are not owing to inconsistencies in the handling of Endymion's transformation. Though Judy Little, *Keats as a Narrative Poet* (Lincoln: University of Nebraska Press, 1975), does not make the distinction between Endymion's conscious and unconscious growth, she argues persuasively that he "has both the Indian Maid and Cynthia, since they are one" (p. 57).

7. Stuart Curran, *Shelley's Annus Mirabilis* (San Marino, Calif.: Huntington Library, 1975), pp. 199–205.

8. For dramatic confirmation of relative frequency of use of the term "death," see *A Concordance to the Writings of William Blake*, 2 vols., ed. David V. Erdman (Ithaca, N.Y.: Cornell University Press, 1967).

9. *Jerusalem*, 80:16–26.

10. *The Four Zoas*, 117: 1, 5–6.

11. *The Four Zoas*, 109: 32–34.

12. Thomas R. Frosch, *The Awakening of Albion* (Ithaca, N.Y.: Cornell University Press, 1974), offers an epitome of this view: "Blake's goal in *Jerusalem* is to wean us from an ethics of mutual forgiveness. As he presents it, forgiveness is less a moral principle contrary to accusation than a radical abandonment of moralism" (p. 91).

13. *Jerusalem*, 38:12–14.

14. *Jerusalem*, 34:30–34.

15. *Jerusalem*, 34:17–19.

16. "Then Jesus appeared standing by Albion as the Good Shepherd / ... & Albion saw his Form / A Man. & they conversed as Man with Man, in Ages of Eternity / And the Divine Appearance was the likeness & similitude of Los" (*Jerusalem*, 96:3–7). "The footsteps of the Lamb of God were there: but now no more / No more shall I behold him, he is closed in Luvahs Sepulcher" (*Jerusalem*, 24:50–51).

17. Susan Fox, *Poetic Form in Blake's "Milton"* (Princeton, N.J.: Princeton University Press, 1976), identifies Blake's solution to the problem: "Multiple perspective and simultaneity [of action, to which Blake the artist is committed] do not in themselves control the structure of *Milton*. If they were the sole ordering devices of the poem, however conscientiously and philosophically devised, they would ensure a work of the most delirious chaos.... The principle that organizes the perspective and repetitions of *Milton* is a framework of parallels at once general and exact" (p. 20).

18. *Milton*, 24:68–76.

19. *Milton*, 22:18–25.

20. *Jerusalem*, 98:38.

21. *A Vision of the Last Judgment* [Page 87].

22. Frosch puts it well: "In Blake sexual desire is ultimately a desire for a non-natural paradise.... What the progression depends upon is a rise from genitality, which cannot be called a sublimation because it is a rise from genital satisfaction and even seems to be inspired by it" (p. 176). Mark Bracher, *Being Form'd—Thinking through Blake's "Milton"* (Barrytown, N.Y.: Station Hill Press, 1985), with special reference to *Milton*, puts the matter of commingling this way: "Fulfillment is ultimately impossible within the realm of immediate presence, for every individual

must eventually perish and lose its immediate actuality forever. The only permanence possible, then, must be a mediated permanence—a permanence of indirect actualization through incorporation of one's own uniqueness into the unique, intrinsic being of other individuals" (p. 104). Would such incorporation improve or diminish the integrity of unique being, might seem a real question; surely "more" being would be in "good" use in such an incorporated condition. And in such a condition, what is "incorporated uniqueness" but "well deployed" individuality? Obviously the categories these crucial terms appear to identify—"individual," "unique," "incorporation," "permanence," "actualization"—are not fixed by discrete meanings; they rather enjoy a "vital instability" to which we are called upon to be sympathetic. See also Bracher, p. 193, for other of the author's views on redemption.

23. *Jerusalem,* 59:50–52.
24. *Visions of the Daughters of Albion,* I:5–17.
25. *Milton,* 18:4–25.
26. *Jerusalem,* 61:1–46.
27. *Jerusalem,* 29:35–30:2.
28. *Jerusalem,* 22:26, 43:33–43.
29. *Milton,* 13:40.
30. *Jerusalem,* 80:16–17, 23–26.
31. *The Four Zoas,* 4:15.
32. *Jerusalem,* 54:12.
33. *Jerusalem,* 4:7.

Index